NURTURING
PROFESSIONAL
JUDGEMENT

Critical Guides for
Teacher Educators

DEDICATION

For Edward and Harry
May all your teachers exercise sound professional judgement.

To order our books please go to our website www.criticalpublishing.com or contact our distributor Ingram Publisher Services, telephone 01752 202301 or email IPSUK.orders@ingramcontent.com. Details of bulk order discounts can be found at www.criticalpublishing.com/delivery-information.

Our titles are also available in electronic format: for individual use via our website and for libraries and other institutions from all the major ebook platforms.

NURTURING
PROFESSIONAL
JUDGEMENT

Series Editor: Ian Menter

Critical Guides for
Teacher Educators

Ben Knight

First published in 2023 by Critical Publishing Ltd

British Library Cataloguing in Publication Data
A CIP record for this book is available from the British Library

ISBN: 978-1-915080-68-4

This book is also available in the following e-book formats:
EPUB ISBN: 978-1-915080-69-1
Adobe e-book ISBN: 978-1-915080-70-7

Text and cover design by Greensplash
Project management by Newgen Publishing UK

Critical Publishing
3 Connaught Road
St Albans
AL3 5RX

www.criticalpublishing.com

Printed on FSC accredited paper

CONTENTS

ABOUT THE SERIES EDITOR

Ian Menter is the former President of BERA, 2013–15. At Oxford University's Department of Education, he was Director of Professional Programmes and led the development of the Oxford Education Deanery. Prior to that he was Professor of Teacher Education at the University of Glasgow and held posts at the University of the West of Scotland, London Metropolitan University, University of the West of England and the University of Gloucestershire. Ian was President of the Scottish Educational Research Association from 2005 to 2007 and chaired the Research and Development Committee of the Universities' Council for the Education of Teachers (UCET) from 2008 to 2011. He is a Visiting Professor at Bath Spa University and Ulster University, and an Honorary Professor at the University of Exeter.

ABOUT THE AUTHOR

Dr Ben Knight has been a teacher educator in higher education since 2009 and before that was a primary school teacher and a senior leader in both suburban and inner-city schools. His research and publications reflect his interest in the complexities of classroom learning, teacher professional development and encouraging teachers to refine and draw on their professional instincts, judgement and intuition.

FOREWORD

Teachers are not machines. They are human beings with enormous responsibility towards the learners they are working with. They have agency (Priestley et al, 2015). Each and every day they are making judgements in response to the demands facing them in their classrooms, schools and colleges. In this book, drawing on considerable experience as a school teacher, a school leader and more recently, as a teacher educator and researcher, Ben Knight explores what is meant by the deceptively simple term *teacher judgement*. He shows how it is possible to develop skills and expertise so that teachers' judgements may become fully professional. At the core of his persuasive argument is the suggestion that there are two main kinds of judgements that teachers need to make. There are those that are planned and considered both in preparation for and in reflection on teaching – what you might call the before and after judgements. However, because of the unpredictable and existential nature of actual teaching, a second type of judgement is also needed, for those decisions that must be made in situ in the classroom. And while, as he suggests, there must necessarily be an element of improvisation in these (he draws an analogy with jazz), he is committed to the view that effective teacher education and mentor support can improve the quality of these apparently spontaneous judgements for the beginning teacher. He categorises these two types of judgement as *Judgement 1* and *Judgement 2*.

In Chapter 3, Ben notes that Shulman (2004, p 504) describes teaching, somewhat dramatically, as *'perhaps the most complex, most challenging, and most demanding, subtle, nuanced and frightening activity that our species ever invented'*. Ben suggests that this is a somewhat exaggerated statement, but that nevertheless it captures something of the essence of teaching that he is seeking to address. He also notes that various commentators and scholars have seen teaching as variously an art, a craft or a science. Ben demonstrates through his own scholarship, and from the experience that he draws on, that it has elements of all three and suggests it may be unhelpful to ascribe teaching to only one of these terms. The approach he takes in the book aligns closely to what Burn and her colleagues have examined under the heading of practical theorising (Burn et al, 2023) and to the development of teachers' adaptive expertise.

The book will be invaluable to teacher educators and beginning teachers as they come to terms with the demands of the simultaneously challenging, fascinating and rewarding occupation they have chosen. It is a great addition to our series and complements several of the other volumes already published.

Ian Menter
Series Editor, Critical Guides for Teacher Educators
Emeritus Professor of Teacher Education, University of Oxford

CHAPTER 1 | INTRODUCTION

In their book *Teaching as a Subversive Activity*, Neil Postman and Charles Weingartner (1969) noted that the latter half of the twentieth century appeared to be changing more rapidly than during all preceding periods of human history. They cited rapid developments in technology, human connectedness, developments in social values and human movement. They pointed out that it was becoming increasingly difficult for people to keep up with the rate of change. In short, change was changing. This process has continued (and may be intensifying) into the twenty-first century where change continues to accelerate at a dizzying pace. At the same time, as many of the activities and processes which govern our lives are becoming increasingly routinised, automated and instant through new technologies, many of the challenges which current school pupils will face when they reach adulthood are shaping up to be seemingly intractable, interconnected and extremely complex. This places considerable responsibility on education systems which will need to prepare young people to develop new approaches to problem-solving, system thinking habits and increasing comfort with uncertainty. Their teachers too will need to possess these skills and dispositions because, despite impressive developments in artificial intelligence and machine learning, one activity that will never become automated (at least where human learning is concerned) is teaching.

Human learning, particularly in groups or classrooms (and perhaps especially where children and young people are concerned), is simply too complex to be reliably routinised to the extent that artificial intelligence could manage the task. To that end, we will always need teachers. Not only that, but those teachers will need to be capable and comfortable operating within increasing complexity. Like in many professions, teachers do not simply repeat the same tasks in the same ways moment by moment, or day by day because as Tom (1980, p 317) eloquently put it:

educational phenomena are not the kind of natural phenomena which under careful study reveal law-like relationships among variables

and because of this,

there are no logical [...] reasons for believing that every educational problem has one best solution.

Teaching and learning situations comprise complex, uniquely configured events which demand continual expert, context-sensitive responses. In short, they require expert professional judgement.

According to Berliner (2004), experts are self-regulatory, whereas novices – who are the focus of this book – require degrees of external regulation in the form of questioning, reflection and reality checks to encourage the development of professional judgement. This book is predicated on the assumption that the skills and dispositions associated with professional judgement do not simply develop on their own; they are elicited and gradually transformed through a combination of reflection, coaching, challenge, guidance and modelling. This book focuses attention on the ways teacher educators and school-based mentors can facilitate these opportunities for pre-service and novice teachers to help them achieve this. In the book, I argue that developing professional judgement *is* developing as a teacher because sound judgement, expert teaching and successful learning go hand in hand. I posit that there is virtually no distinction between what it means to become an expert teacher and what it means to become expert at making classroom and learning-related judgements. Expert teachers are necessarily accomplished at making judgements about their work and their pupils' learning. The reason for this, I argue, is that there is no facet of teachers' work which, done well, does not rely on exercising judgement. It follows therefore that pre-service and novice teachers who take steps to improve their judgements will also be improving their overall teaching expertise.

How can novices set about developing the repertoire of skills and attributes associated with the development of teacher judgement? Reflective individuals will, to a minimal extent, build capacities for judgement through their everyday practice, not quite by osmosis, but perhaps with little deliberate effort. Residual developments in many skills and dispositions can be expected to occur to varying degrees unconsciously through action. I argue that to be more deliberate, and surer, about developing professional judgement, however, expert teacher education and classroom mentoring should become more explicitly judgement-focused. This would accelerate developments in professional practice by bringing into relief processes, skills and dispositions which may otherwise remain largely tacit. In this book, I present frameworks for thinking about and interpreting classroom incidents as well as guidance for teacher educators and school mentors about ways of supporting novices in becoming consciously competent in their judgements.

Contents of this book

The book begins by exploring and defining the key concepts associated with the development of teacher judgement. Following this, it wrestles with the reasons why judgement is such an integral part of successful teaching. This centres on the inherent complexity of classrooms and the complex relationship between teaching and learning. Next, I explore ways in which teacher educators and school-based mentors might support novice teachers to grapple with that complexity, develop some comfort with uncertainty and learn to make useful and productive judgements about their teaching and pupils' learning. I present a range of case studies drawn from the experiences of real pre-service teachers, novice teachers, university tutors and school-based mentors, and analyse their struggles and successes in building and supporting the development of professional judgement.

Throughout the book, I have distinguished between two different categories of judgement and refer to these as *judgement 1* and *judgement 2* (see Figure 1.1 below). *Judgement 1* relates to the reasoning and decision making in which teachers engage before and after teaching events, typically while planning for or evaluating lessons and learning. *Judgement 1* occurs away from the live moment of teaching where there is more time for reflection and contemplation on prior (and possible future) classroom events. *Judgement 1* maps loosely onto Schön's (1983) well-known concept of reflection *on* action. *Judgement 2* occurs while immersed in the moment of teaching. *Judgement 2*'s judgements are quicker, more instinctive and more intuitive than *judgement 1*'s judgements and map loosely onto Schön's notion of reflection *in* action. Like all complex activities, teaching is not easily compartmentalisable, and therefore the line between *in* and *on* the moment is not always clear. However, a useful way of thinking about these two manifestations of judgement is decisions made first while away from learners (*judgement 1*) and second while with learners (*judgement 2*). Reflection plays a pivotal mediating role in the exercising of sound professional judgement; however, I have tried to separate this from judgement itself. In this book, professional judgement refers to the decisions and decisional capacity, both *on* and *in* the moment of teaching which result from, among other things, reflection. Models for *judgements 1* and *2* are presented in Chapters 2 and 4, and then discussed together in Chapter 5.

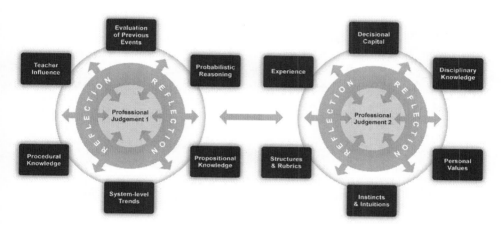

Figure 1.1 The two categories of professional judgement

Judgement in teaching requires the collision and integration of propositional and procedural knowledge. That is, knowledge (or at least a priori assumptions) that something is the case and knowledge (or at least reasonable predictions) about what is required to do or achieve something. Ultimately, teaching is about doing. However, knowledge about how to teach, what to do and how best to do it in the service of learning relies on the phenomenological experience of operating, reasoning, and deciding in the classroom *and* on statistically and theoretically derived knowledge about how learning emerges and the likely consequences of particular teacher actions. Teachers can, and should, draw reasonable inferences from the wealth of theoretical knowledge about teaching and learning to inform their judgements. They can, and should, also reflect on their teaching experiences, including the successes and the failures. This means that, as Winch et al (2015, p 202) note, teachers must develop a constructive view of educational research and its products, aiming for what they describe as a '*research-based textured notion of professional judgement*'.

My starting point when writing this book was that debates about the supremacy of different conceptions of teaching as a craft (Rogers, 2016; Grimmett and MacKinnon, 1992), art (Fraher, 1984) or applied science (Tomlinson, 1997; Thorndike, 1910) are largely unavailing. Convincing arguments can be made for each, because teaching is all these things. This is perhaps the main reason why it is so difficult to determine what good teaching looks like. Should we judge it as art, craft or science? Should we assess its values base and moral outcomes, its creativity, its processes or its products? Add to this the contextual uniqueness of every classroom and the interactions within them and it is not difficult to see why Jordan et al (2014) describe teaching as complicated. In fact (as they also acknowledge), it is more than just complicated, it is complex (see Chapter 3 for a discussion of the difference) and complex phenomena are resistant to simple breakdown, description or standardisation. The often tacit, unpredictable, indeterminate and contingent nature of learning means that teachers cannot simply follow a script or duplicate rules or procedures. The praxis at the heart of teaching demands that they draw on multiple sources of propositional and procedural knowledge in order to judge what is best. This idea lies at the heart of this book.

Who is this book for?

The audience for the book is university-based teacher educators and school-based mentors who guide novices during early career stages. However, I hope its insights will also appeal to trainee and novice teachers to whom it regularly refers. In places, the content of the book is directed specifically to those preparing pre-service teachers, at other times it is aimed specifically at those mentoring new teachers, and sometimes it is for both. When writing about pre-service teachers I often use the term *trainee* for ease (though I see teacher education as so much more than merely *training*) and when referring to early career teachers I tend to use the term *novice*. Occasionally, for grammatical succinctness, I use the term *novice* to refer to both pre-service and early career teachers and I hope the context makes the distinction clear.

In over 25 years, first as a classroom teacher, school senior leader and subsequently a teacher educator and educational researcher, I have had the distinct pleasure of nurturing the professional judgement of numerous new and aspiring teachers. I'm not sure I have always performed this role perfectly; I hope I have done it well more often than not. However, it has always been immensely satisfying to support young professionals on that important journey towards teacher expertise, the process of which has convinced me that teaching is essentially about making judgements. Sometimes these are quick and instinctive, sometimes slow and reasoned, but either way the capacity to make useful and productive judgements in teaching requires time, rehearsal, space for mistakes and missteps, professional dialogue and most crucially reflection. As facilitators of all these opportunities, teacher educators and early career mentors play a pivotal role in creating the conditions in which judgement can emerge, blossom productively and become habitual.

One of the obstacles to achieving this, and perhaps a reason why this book feels necessary, is that in England and comparable education systems, professional judgement is conspicuous by its near complete absence from policies governing teacher education and early career development. The top-down nature of educational change at national levels means that anything out of sight in policy frameworks remains frustratingly out of mind too. I elaborate on this theme in Chapter 5 and suggest some practical, and reasonably minor, changes to teacher education policy and curriculum, as well as early career frameworks, which would bring judgement more into relief in teacher development. While the primary audiences for the book are teacher educators, early career mentors, trainee and novice teachers, it also makes overtures to policymakers to consider the benefits of a subtle shift away from outcomes towards more process-driven policy.

CHAPTER 2 | WHAT IS PROFESSIONAL JUDGEMENT AND WHY IS IT IMPORTANT FOR NOVICE TEACHERS?

CRITICAL ISSUES

- *What defines professionalism? Are there actions, capabilities and expectations typically associated with being a qualified teacher?*
- *What about professional licence? Should teachers enjoy permissions typically afforded to other professionals?*
- *What is it about teaching which makes judgement so important?*
- *What forms do professional judgements take in the context of teaching?*
- *Is it reasonable to expect pre-service and novice teachers to develop capacities for professional judgement?*
- *Can professional judgement be taught?*

Introduction

In Chapter 1 I noted that much of what goes on in classrooms is tacit, that is to say, not obvious or immediately evident. This is true for some of the mechanisms from which learning arises and which produce classroom cultures, ethos and social dynamics. Another way of expressing this is to say that these and other classroom phenomena have emergent qualities; a life of their own to some extent. Following on from this, I argued that managing tacit phenomena requires teachers to draw upon more than simple rules and rubrics; to be successful they must also develop instincts and intuitions in order to make judgements about the classroom, about pupil behaviours, interactions and learning. In short, teaching is complex, and in complex situations it is rare for solutions to present themselves without the need for judgement. In this chapter, I build on this by exploring what professional judgement is and why it is important for soon-to-be and novice teachers.

The nature of professionalism

Expectations placed on professionals tend to fall quite neatly into two categories. The first, which will be immediately recognised by many from within and outside of the teaching profession, relates to expectations for professional conduct. Professionals are expected to behave in certain ways (and avoid behaving in certain ways). This conception of professionalism is typically guided by rubrics setting out minimum standards deemed necessary to uphold public trust in institutions and their associated professions. This category of professionalism is important but is not the principal focus of this book. The second category, and the main focus of this book, interprets professionalism slightly differently, being more concerned with describing how members of a given profession are expected to act in order to successfully fulfil their responsibilities. I have previously described this conception of professionalism as centring on ideas about both licence and capacity (Witt et al, 2022). Professionalism in this sense tends to come with expectations that professionals are both permitted to and capable of enacting, or capitalising on, any of the following.

» *Disciplinary knowledge* – what a professional knows about their discipline and ways to apply that knowledge.

» *Subjective discretionary judgement* – a professional independently acting to change, improve or try out approaches without direction or supervision.

» *Situational sensitivity* – how professionals perceive and interpret events before choosing a course of action.

» *Professional instinct or intuition* – when professionals just know that something needs attending to, changing, revising or discarding altogether, the trigger for which is often subtle or barely perceptible.

» *Decisional capital* – a form of professional cachet, or seal of approval, enabling professionals to confidently make executive decisions about their work.

In professions such as law, medicine or social work, among others, it is usual to think of the professional as being expected to exercise their judgement about situations which arise in the course of their work. In fact, clients would expect it. Situational judgement tends to be naturally associated with such professions (Brest and Hamilton-Krieger, 2010; Hargreaves and Fullan, 2012; Taylor and Whittaker, 2018) because they operate in complex, nuanced and grey areas, where solutions rely as much on interpretation as on protocol. Expectations on teachers tend to be less clear-cut and despite consistently being seen by the public as among the most trusted professionals in society (86 per cent, second only to doctors in the UK; Ipsos MORI, 2015), many in the profession, while feeling capable of judging what is best in their classrooms, do not feel as permitted as they would like to exercise the sort of discretionary judgement that is routinely welcomed in other professional fields (NFER, 2020). The reasons for this are complex, some of which are explored in Chapter 5, but for now, let us maintain the focus on what professionalism looks like in the context of teaching.

The professional conduct aspects of teaching are most evident in professional standards and expectations. Over the last 40 years in the UK, there have been many iterations and revisions of professional rubrics issued by successive governments (for an overview, see Knight, 2017), the most recent being the Teachers' Standards (TS) (DfE, 2011), all of which articulate variations on similar themes about the minimum standards of teacher competency and conduct. Comparable education systems across the world have their own professionalism rubrics. For example, Australia has the Professional Standards for Teachers (PST) (AITSL, 2018), New Zealand has the Code of Professional Responsibility (CPR) and Standards for the Teaching Profession (STP), and Canada has the federalised Professional Standards for Educators (PSE) across the different Canadian states (eg Alberta Education, 2023). These all share many similarities while also being distinct in their own ways. These represent one side of the professionalism coin, so to speak, and form the basis against which pre-service teachers are often assessed for professional status and against which existing teachers' performance is appraised. Disciplinary matters may also be settled by applying such rubrics. There is plenty to critique about the form and content of such frameworks (Hulme and Quirk-Marku, 2017 and Sinnema et al, 2017 offer thorough interrogations); however, they are necessary for holding teachers to account for the quality of their professional work and help sustain public trust in education. And, while they do influence other aspects of teacher professionalism, not least because they risk undermining them in some ways, they are not the main focus of this book.

The main focus of this book and the other side of the professionalism coin are those aspects which depend on teachers being able to draw on certain expertise in response to the complexity of everyday classroom teaching and learning. In many ways, teaching is very much like the professions mentioned earlier in this chapter, which operate in tacit, interpretive and indeterminate spheres. Teaching is also full of grey areas. Teaching and learning are complex phenomena, so it is no surprise that the professional work of teachers involves more than simply following predetermined protocols and procedures. Schön (1987, p 4) described teaching as operating in the 'swampy lowlands' of everyday life, an analogy many teachers will find no difficulty relating to I am sure. Schön's implication, that the way ahead is not always immediately clear and that what worked last time, might not work next time, will ring true for anyone who has attempted to teach a class of pupils. When we cannot see where we are going (as in a swampy lowland), road maps such as professional descriptors and lesson plans are essential, but we also typically feel our way, and this is where teacher professional judgement comes in. This basic principle was at the heart of the various books Schön authored: objective certainties (what he termed 'technical rationalism') could not provide all the answers for how practitioners should operate. Judgement, enabled by reflective practice, is also essential. Let us look at how Schön's ideas sit alongside other related assertions about professional judgement.

What the literature says about teacher professional judgement

» Schön (1987, p 4) explained that 'the problems of real-world practice do not present themselves to practitioners as well-formed structures. Indeed, they do not tend to present themselves as problems at all, but as messy indeterminate situations'.

» In a similar vein, Hargreaves and Fullan (2012, p 107) posit that 'uncertainty is the parent of professionalism'. Because uncertainty is in its very nature, teaching calls for 'wise, well-founded judgement'.

» Hoyle and John (1995, p 77) built on Schön's ideas suggesting that since professionals (including teachers) 'work in uncertain situations', 'judgement is more important than routine'.

» Similarly, Tripp (1993, p 13) focuses on the relationship between routine and judgement in arguing that the *'strength of routines is that they enable us to do things without consciously attending to them, that is also their danger [...] to develop professional judgement, we have to move beyond our everyday "working" way of looking at things'*.

» Heilbronn (2008, p 103) notes that teachers' professional judgements are inevitably subjective, explaining that *'since experiences are personal, even if there were a body of standardised knowledge about good teacher behaviour, it could not be passed down in the form of a technical manual. Each teacher experiences her place of work or study through her own meaning-making. These personal experiences are the ground on which practical judgement builds and is connected to action'*.

» Dewey (1960, p 245) saw teacher judgement as a product of *'intelligent action'*. He described the ability to make fluent and useful judgements about classroom events as the *'selection and arrangement of means to effect consequences'*, noting that *'intelligence is as practical as reason is theoretical'*.

» Furlong (2000) argues that there are three key dimensions to teacher professionalism: *specialist knowledge*, *autonomy* and *responsibility*. *'It is because professionals face complex and unpredictable situations that they need a* specialist body of knowledge; *if they are to apply that knowledge [...] they need the* autonomy *to make judgements; and given that they have autonomy, it is essential that they act with* responsibility*'*.

» Claxton (2000, p 40) sees judgement as one of the small suite of dispositions (or *'ways of knowing'*) which lack *'clearly articulated comprehension or rationale'*. For him, teacher judgements involve *'making accurate decisions and categorisations without, at the time, being able to explain or justify them'*.

» Lizzio and Wilson (2007) argue that *'one of the fundamental goals of professional education should be developing the capacity for professional judgement: the ability to confidently act in "no right answer" (Schön, 1983), or "unfamiliar and changing" circumstances (Stephenson and Weil, 1992)'*.

A few essential ideas link these assertions about and explanations of teacher judgement. I have separated them into two categories, beginning with those which justify the need for teachers to make judgements, followed by assertions about the nature of successful judgement-making.

Category 1

» Teaching is complex and therefore full of uncertainty (explored further in Chapter 3).

» Uncertainty renders routines and rubrics, at best, only partially useful.

» Because of this, judgement is an essential ingredient in teacher action.

Category 2

» Professional judgements are multi-faceted, sometimes tacit and draw on different domains of professional experience.

» Judgement is subjective and a teacher's attitudes and values are central to the judgements they make.

» Developments in professional judgement can (and should) be scaffolded through teaching and mentoring.

We return to each of these themes at various points in the book, but for now it is worth asking what teacher judgements typically look like, and what all this implies for pre-service and novice teachers, as well as for those who teach and mentor them.

Ideas about teacher professional judgements

One prominent conception of teacher judgement comes from Tripp (1993), who designates four categories of judgments which he describes in the following ways.

1. *Practical judgement* is the basis of every action taken in the conduct of teaching, and the majority of which is made instantly.

2. *Diagnostic judgement* involves using profession-specific knowledge and academic expertise to recognise, describe, understand, explain and interpret judgements.

3. *Reflective judgement* concerns more personal and moral judgements involving the identification, description, exploration and justification of the judgements made and values implicit and espoused in practical (teaching) decisions and their explanations.

4. *Critical judgement*, through formal investigation, involves challenge to and evaluation of the judgements and values revealed by reflection.

Tripp asserts that some of these forms of judgement come more naturally to most teachers than others, and that while all teachers develop degrees of practical judgement, largely through experience, few engage in the sort of analytical thinking required for diagnostic judgement because reflecting upon and understanding the origins and consequences of practical judgements take time and expertise. As a minimum, Tripp suggests that teachers must '*think about their practice*' (p 140), but he lays responsibility for novices developing diagnostic and critical judgement at the feet of teacher education. We revisit this idea in Chapter 5. In a previous book in this series, Tony Eaude (2012) situated professional judgement as a facet of teacher expertise, describing teacher judgements as being either long term (concerning future events) or in the moment (concerning the here and now). These categories loosely correlate with Schön's (1991) notions of reflection both *on* and *in* practice. In this book, for ease, I refer to the former as professional judgement type 1 and the latter as professional judgement type 2. Professional judgement 1 involves looking ahead and planning for future action, taking account of the range of known and unknown factors to judge the best approach. For teachers, this is seen most in long-, medium- and short-term lesson planning, creating or adapting resources and grouping children for activities, whereby reflection on events and outcomes of previous lessons provides points of reference for reasoning about a range of factors in future lessons. In contrast, Eaude's in-the-moment judgements (professional judgement 2) are essentially improvisations which adjust the course of classroom action in pursuit of optimal conditions for teaching and learning. This distinction between in situ and pre or post facto judgements is also evident in the distinctions between the practical and reflective judgements in Tripp's model.

Winch et al (2015) see teacher judgement as an aspect of professional knowledge. They draw on the concepts of 'tacit knowledge' and 'phronesis' to describe how teachers become able to 'grasp the salient features of a situation' (p 5) and engage in intuitive decision making about the best courses of action. Along with others, they assert that teachers make longer-term and in situ judgements by drawing on different aspects of professional knowledge, including theoretical, technical and reflective. They do this by integrating their understanding of what research suggests has proved most effective in the past with the technical skills they have developed to date, their subject knowledge and what reflection on their own and others' practice has taught them. There is some consensus that these strands of professional knowledge must operate in concert if teachers are to make useful and productive judgements about their work. This of course, is no mean feat for novice teachers, or indeed for those responsible for designing and implementing teacher education programmes. Chapter 5 looks in more detail at ways teacher education and teacher educators might do more to emphasise these aspects of professional development.

What does this mean for pre-service and early career teachers?

Running throughout the literature on teacher professionalism and the development of professional judgement are the assertions that (1) judgements are not made in a vacuum (ie they are always about or in relation to something) and (2) that experience is a key driver of their development. Considering that pre-service teachers spend a good deal of their training programmes not in school and that, on the whole, their classroom experience prior to becoming qualified is fairly limited, it is valid to ask how they might realistically go about rehearsing, using and developing their professional judgements. Picking up on Furlong's point above, another challenge facing pre-service teachers in particular, though early career teachers as well to some extent, is their characteristic lack of autonomy. While always positioned as visitors, always teaching in another teacher's classroom, necessarily subordinate to their professional mentors and operating under regular monitoring and scrutiny, exercising discretionary judgement feels like a risk to many trainees, even where they may feel permitted or expected to do so. As I and colleagues have previously noted, the supportive 'structures for assessing pre-service teachers' progress [...] may in fact inhibit the very progress they aim to measure' (Witt et al, 2022, p 9). In addition to these important factors, it is worth remembering that throughout most pre-service teacher training, a reliance on rubrics and routines is (rightly) encouraged as a necessity. The idea of endorsing moves away from the routines and descriptors which typically structure trainee development, and seems somewhat at odds with the objectives of most teacher education programmes.

With all these understandable obstacles to the rehearsal and development of professional judgement, it seems reasonable to ask whether professional judgements are really necessary during teacher education and early career stages. The answer to this question also lies in the literature cited above. Common to those texts, and evident within all discussions about the development of teacher judgement, is its ubiquity and necessity. It is scarcely possible to identify an aspect of teachers' work that does not rely on judgement. Table 2.1 shows (in no particular order) a few examples of the many judgements teachers and pre-service teachers might routinely make. This list only includes a small number of headline judgements and, as such, barely scratches the surface of the myriad judgements teachers may make in a typical day. Each of the judgements in Table 2.1 has a range of micro-judgements behind it and each also acts as an antecedent to new judgements, large and small. Teacher professional judgement is a complex affair.

Table 2.1 Examples of typical judgements made by experienced and trainee teachers.

Teacher judgements	Pre-service/novice teacher judgements
Pitching of lesson content	Pitching of lesson content
Student learning	Student learning
When students are/are not grasping concepts	When students are/are not grasping concepts
Pace of activities and lessons	Pace of activities and lessons
When to/when not to intervene	When to/when not to intervene
How to scaffold learning and when to withdraw	How to scaffold learning and when to withdraw
How to motivate learners	How to motivate learners
What questions to ask, how to pose them and when to ask them	What questions to ask, how to pose them and when to ask them
Appropriate responses to unexpected events (sudden behavioural challenges, outbreaks of humour, wasps flying into the classroom, snow)	Appropriate responses to unexpected events (sudden behavioural challenges, outbreaks of humour, wasps flying into the classroom, snow)

(*continued*)

Table 2.1 (*Cont.*)

Teacher judgements	Pre-service/novice teacher judgements
Maintaining student focus and engagement	Maintaining student focus and engagement
Regaining student focus and engagement	Regaining student focus and engagement
When student alertness is fading	When student alertness is fading
Wording/rewording explanations	Wording/rewording explanations
Centralising or distributing classroom control	Centralising or distributing classroom control
Capitalising when new learning is emerging	Capitalising when new learning is emerging
Deploying/redeploying adult support	Deploying/redeploying adult support
Managing student conflict	Managing student conflict
When individual tasks need to be made easier/harder	When individual tasks need to be made easier/harder
Whether the classroom is too noisy	Whether the classroom is too noisy
Whether to include, modify or skip planned content	Whether to include, modify or skip planned content
When a student needs encouragement/ when a student needs a firm reminder	When a student needs encouragement/ when a student needs a firm reminder

You will notice immediately that both lists are identical. This is because there is no classroom judgement expected of experienced teachers which pre-service and early career teachers are not also required to rehearse, develop and hone. More experienced teachers might notice the need for judgements more readily and apply them more instinctively, but since all the above judgements (and the myriad not mentioned) directly or indirectly influence pupil learning, it seems reasonable to expect pre-service and early career teachers to cultivate the skills and dispositions necessary to develop this area of teacher expertise. Whether, considering issues discussed in preceding paragraphs, teacher education programmes can create conditions conducive to this is discussed later in this book. The following case study, however, illustrates how some of the above judgements might be required of a pre-service teacher during teaching practicum. While reading it, look out for judgements from the above list which the trainee makes and consider the factors which prompted them.

CASE **STUDY**

Professional judgement during an extended teaching practicum

Luke is a final year pre-service teacher on a three-year undergraduate initial teacher education degree programme at a British university. A few weeks into his final placement in a lively urban class, he encounters the following typical scenario during a morning mathematics lesson.

The lesson begins with a short period of direct instruction in which Luke explains the intended learning for the lesson and briefly recaps how this will build on learning from the previous few lessons. Through questioning, he judges that several pupils have not retained key concepts from the previous lessons and so he decides to spend a few extra minutes revising these. He then introduces the new method for the current lesson but realising that some pupils will not be able to complete the activities he planned for today due to lack of understanding, he decides on the spot to work more with these pupils and to ask the others to begin working on their warm-up tasks. He asks his teaching assistant (TA) (whom he had planned to support two particular pupils) to supervise this transition and ensure the pupils settle quickly into their activities while he works with the pupils who require more support. There is some fuss and disruption which requires his intervention, so he and the TA agree to swap roles momentarily and the TA works with his small group while Luke establishes calm among the rest of the class. The TA then begins working with their designated pupils and Luke resumes teaching his small group, eventually sending them to their table groups to undertake the planned tasks.

Later in the lesson, Luke follows his lesson plan and checks the pupils' learning of a number concept by asking the class some informal assessment questions and inviting them to show with their thumbs up or down how well they have understood. For one such question, only three pupils put their thumbs up to indicate that they have understood, all other thumbs are down. He decides that he could support all pupils by asking the three who have understood to come to the front and invite those who have not to ask them questions. This was not on his lesson plan, but this way all pupils have the potential to learn and be challenged. He reinforces this by organising a physical demonstration of the number concept using a range of pupils from all groups. This was also not on his plan but occurred to him in the moment. Judging that enough pupils have now shown they understand the concept and realising that they will not have time to complete all the tasks he set, he tells all pupils to complete the task that they are on, before closing their books and waiting for the next instruction.

This short episode will resonate with most teachers. The trainee made a range of judgements about pupil understanding, logistics, lesson pace, personnel, pupil engagement, task pitch and scope, and lesson plan flexibility. This is the everyday stuff of teaching. It could be argued that some of these in-the-moment judgements were prompted by poor lesson planning, and a reflective teacher will always consider whether a better plan would have avoided the need for certain improvised decisions. However, as we have seen in the literature, classrooms and the pupils in them can be unpredictable which means even experienced teachers' lesson plans do not always accurately anticipate everything which may transpire during lessons.

A few notable characteristics of judgement-making are evident in this short case study. First, improvised deviations from lesson plans, such as those made by Luke, are not rare or unusual events. On the contrary, they are daily occurrences in most classrooms which has led Dezutter (2011, p 27), among others, to describe teaching as *inherently improvisational*. The requirement for teachers to improvise varies from lesson to lesson and from day to day, but improvisation in one form or another is ever-present. Second, that judgements tend to beget judgements. Having rightly judged it necessary to deviate from his plan to meet the specific needs of a small group of pupils, Luke was confronted with new judgements to make about logistics, deploying adult support, pacing and timings. This experience is frequently reported by jazz musicians and unscripted actors (Holdhus et al, 2016), who describe how when they improvise, each novel extemporization leads to further ad-libs and so on, as a knock-on effect of spontaneity ensues, requiring more and more in situ judgements. Sawyer (2004, p 13) describes these moments in the classroom as *'disciplined improvisations'* because, while the outcomes of such decisions may not be known, they take place within the broad structures of the lesson and classroom constraints. In this case study, Luke made a series of improvisations (judgement 2) which moved him away from his plans, but he subsequently managed to manoeuvre back to them, much like how a jazz musician repeatedly deviates from and returns to a main motif. Third, to varying degrees, each judgement made, including those relating to timing and logistics, influenced pupil learning. Looking at the judgements Luke made, it is evident that whether directly or indirectly, each decision had consequences for all pupils, their tasks, levels of support and eventual learning.

The pre-service teacher in this case study demonstrated high levels of expertise to notice and respond to the unexpected and adjust his actions accordingly. However, such responsiveness first requires the autonomy to act (agency) and sufficient licence to decide (decisional capital) which, as previously discussed, are not often granted to or prevalent in trainees. Next, he required sufficient situational sensitivity and instinct to help him interpret events in order to then make discretionary judgements. Finally, he needed to be constantly reflecting on the consequences of his judgements and adjusting in light of his interpretation of events. Bringing these elements together during lessons is not easy and while it is tempting to presume that these skills simply develop with experience, some have begun to consider whether, and how, more concerted efforts might be made to integrate these skills and dispositions explicitly into teacher education. For example, Philip (2019, p 2), acknowledging the importance of experience, argues that teacher education should prioritise experiences which *'centre improvisation and the inherent uncertainty, ambiguity and unpredictability of teaching'*. Similarly, Lobman (2011) and Dezutter (2011) have made the case that improvisation is a required skill for teacher development and that teacher educators should support their students to recognise and respond to this fact. Mæland and Espeland (2017), who conducted research into novice teachers' conceptions of improvisation in teaching in Norway, concluded that improvisation should be seen as a key professional skill and should be included in teacher education curricula, in the context of teachers' responsibility, accountability and autonomy. In Chapter 5 we will explore how this might be achieved.

Anatomy of professional judgement: how do pre-service and novice teachers develop it?

Arguments about why professional judgements, long-term or improvised, are important skills for pre-service teachers to develop centre mostly on the assertion that like other dynamic, shifting, not entirely predictable domains of human action, in some innate ways teaching simply *demands* it. Taking for granted that all schools and school classrooms are to varying degrees characterised by uncertainty, it seems reasonable to want to equip novice teachers with the tools to confidently and fruitfully manage that uncertainty. Heilbronn (2008, p 111) puts it nicely in my view,

Flexibility in response to change and complexity are key characteristics of good teachers because of the non-routinisable dynamic of teaching X to Y. Teaching is not a formulaic activity.

If teaching, like other professional domains, is by its very nature complex and uncertain, I return to a lingering question for teacher education: *'to what extent can we expect pre-service teachers to develop the skills to navigate it?'* For a long time, there have been two broad schools of thought about the development of practical judgement, what is sometimes called *'phronesis'*, within teacher education. There are those who see teaching as a craft and the development of judgement as something which cannot be taught but must instead be mastered on the job. This view has some empirical backing (Lizzio and Wilson, 2004; Kember and Leung, 2005) and underpins the rising number of school-based pathways into the profession. Others see teaching more as an intellectual activity and are less confident that the skills associated with professional judgement will automatically develop through exposure to classroom teaching. This second group view teacher judgement, especially judgement 2, as requiring more explicit nurturing through teaching and engagement with theory and research. This theory-into-practice view predominates in university-based teacher education. In many ways this is a false dichotomy, however, and most teacher educators generally agree that virtually all teacher skills and dispositions benefit from some out-of-context teaching, some knowledge of theory and some contextualised real-world rehearsal and reflection. Helleve et al (2021, p 14) sum this up when they argue that *'student teachers should learn "that" in the university and be able to bring the knowledge to the practice-field and transform it into knowing "how"'*.

However, two things set judgement apart from some other skills novice teachers are required to develop and lend weight to assertions that it is best developed on the job. First, that judgement permeates every other pedagogical competency (it is scarcely possible to think of a teacher action which is not mediated by judgement) and second, that judgements (especially judgement 2) often arise out of instincts, feelings or a *sense* that something is not working and responses to such instincts are often unconscious. Claxton (2000, p 35) refers to this as intuitive practice and explains that,

The expert teacher may go through a whole lesson, adjusting or even abandoning their actions as they go, without being conscious of much reasoning, and without being able to say why or how they made the 'decisions' they did, or to what clues they were responding.

Based on this description, it is not difficult to argue that time spent teaching in classrooms will play a pivotal role in the development of judgement 2. However, as we have already seen, professional judgement has multiple interdependent components and the sort of intuitive capacities Claxton refers to do not exist or develop in isolation from other capacities such as disciplinary knowledge, decisional capital and personal values. In fact, when teachers are *feeling their way* through lessons (a necessary precondition for professional judgement 2), they are likely to be capitalising upon a number of capacities and conditions. I have modelled this coalition of factors in Figure 2.1.

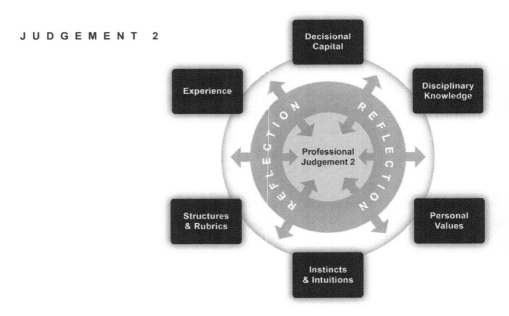

Figure 2.1 Factors contributing to category 2 professional judgements

It seems reasonable to presume that the obvious place for a novice teacher to develop their decisional capital and situational instincts would be in the school classroom (literally in situ[ation]), but the other factors which contribute towards professional judgement 2 according to Figure 2.1 are at least partly, if not largely, developed outside of the classroom.

Disciplinary knowledge, personal values and reflections on action can all be meaningfully supported by effective mentoring in school and effective study and teaching in university. This leads to one of my central arguments in this book that both types of professional judgement, perhaps particularly professional judgement 2, can only develop when nurtured through a combination of classroom practice and effective *pre* and *après* practice teaching and mentoring. A feature of the model in Figure 2.1 is that each of the six contributing factors shares two-way relationships with the development of judgement 2 and are mediated by reflection. This indicates something important about the development of in-the-moment judgement; that as it develops, it also strengthens the factors which develop it, and that this does not necessarily just occur automatically but relies on reflection both *in* and *on* action. Each of the six contributing factors in Figure 2.1 is also mutually influential, something we will explore more in Chapter 4; however, for now, let us focus on their individual contributions to the development of professional judgement 2.

Decisional capital

For pre-service teachers and novices to begin to exercise discretionary judgement, they must feel confident and permitted to do so. Decisional capital is something professionals build over time which unlocks their own internal confidence to act, and others' confidence in them. This presents a challenge for pre-service teachers in particular, because their time spent in classrooms is often brief. It is also time spent in someone else's classroom, meaning that even on longer placements of several weeks or months, a trainee's visitor status never disappears entirely. Building decisional capital in these conditions is not easy. To combat this, trainees and novices need clear, unambiguous signals from their supervising teachers, school mentors and university tutors that, within reasonable limits, they are both permitted and indeed expected to use their judgement in the classroom. Naturally, this permission needs to be carefully structured around a trainee's confidence and capabilities and will look somewhat different from one trainee to the next, and in the early stages of training compared to later on. However, the sense that one has licence to rehearse judgements (even small ones) is an important prerequisite to judgement development. We might say that being able to exercise judgement begins with feeling permitted to do so, and that decisional capital grows in conditions where novices feel they have licence to decide, about some things at least. Increased decisional capital increases judgement rehearsal, which in turn boosts decisional capital.

Disciplinary knowledge

The confidence to improvise arises in no small part from confidence in the subject matter being taught and learned. It is well known that insecure subject knowledge tends to result in pre-service and novice teachers taking fewer risks, deviating less often from lesson plans and maintaining more centralised control during lessons. On the contrary, when trainees are confident in their knowledge of the subject matter they tend to teach more adventurously, feel more comfortable deviating from lesson plans where necessary and hand more control over to pupils. Disciplinary knowledge is broader than just curriculum subject knowledge, however.

It also includes knowledge of the ways pupils learn individually and in groups, including likely obstacles to learning, knowledge about pupils' characteristics, classroom ethos and atmosphere, and ways to assess learning. It also involves, among other things, knowledge about the likely effects of their decisions and actions. Disciplinary knowledge plays a significant role in creating conditions conducive to successful judgement 2.

Personal values

To say that teachers draw regularly on their personal values in the classroom would be an understatement. In fact, we might say that values are dispersed across all six contributing factors in Figure 2.1 and woven intrinsically into all teacher judgements. This is because teaching itself is a values-laden pursuit; as Menter (2016) points out, teaching has an inescapable moral dimension to it. Perhaps the most universal value for all teachers is that all their pupils learn and make progress. Other values, such as doing one's best, kindness, fairness and inclusivity, permeate teachers' work moment by moment as, to some extent, do civic values including democracy, tolerance, the rule of law and individual liberty. Whether taught explicitly or modelled implicitly, such values provide important underpinning for the many varied judgements (types 1 and 2) teachers make. Most teacher judgements are both motivated and influenced to a greater or lesser extent by the values listed above. A challenge for novices may be that values, in their most useful forms, are not handed down on stone tablets, rather they emerge for individuals through their interactions with others and critical engagement with ideas and principles. We might say that values are versatile and emergent, not fixed and conferred. A useful illustration of this is seen in the way the process of rehearsing judgement in the classroom not only is influenced by one's values but also consolidates or adjusts one's values.

Instincts and intuitions

Developing situational sensitivity is central to intuiting when a judgement call is required. Of the six contributing factors in Figure 2.1, this is the one most readily acquired through experience and supported least through *après* practice teaching and mentoring. That is not to say mentoring cannot support its development, but the ability to sense when something needs to change, stop altogether, speed up, slow down, be reconfigured or indeed remain the same is a form of phronesis which comes principally from practical participation in teaching. Pollard (2010, p 5) describes it in the following way '*the more expert a teacher becomes, the more his/her expertise is manifested in sensitivity to contexts and situations, in imaginative judgements in-the-moment sourced from tacit knowledge.*' The implication here is that when a teacher senses that things are not operating optimally in the classroom, they may not be able to articulate from where that sense originated. Knowledge like this – what we sometimes call a hunch – is often felt rather than consciously known and is also often acquired implicitly, what psychologists refer to as unconscious competence. Eraut (2000, p 257) describes intuitive elements in judgement as '*a sense of fitness for purpose which goes beyond logical analysis*'. I can relate to this description because when reflecting back on my time as a class teacher, many of the multitudes of micro-judgements I made each day stemmed from an inkling that something wasn't quite right and I found myself reacting before, or without, reasoning.

Structures and rubrics

Structures including lesson-planning templates and example lesson plans, timetables and curriculum along with rubrics such as professional standards or competencies offer pre-service teachers and novices helpful architecture around which to apply their judgements. Such frameworks are like the safe harbour from which apprentices learn to venture when rehearsing their judgement and to which they subsequently return, perhaps venturing longer and longer over time. The safety which these structures and rubrics offer in this harbour analogy is the distilled prior experiences of others. In the absence of one's own experience, the collective experience of those who have gone before are worthwhile starting points for new teachers to internalise, and from which, in time, they may make their own deviations and take their own risks.

Experience

This is something which pre-service teachers and novices necessarily lack and therefore to some extent it may be the most likely obstacle to their capacity to exercise judgement 2. There is no question that longer-in-service teachers have more of this upon which to draw when forming and exercising judgements. As colleagues and I have previous noted, there is no getting around the problem of experience.

The journey from novice to expert necessarily involves a configuration of common elements; experience, time, reflection and mentoring. These factors cannot be bypassed and, in particular, time cannot be cheated; the novice has to put the hours in.

(Witt et al, 2022, p 8)

Experience enhances one's capacity for exercising judgement primarily because it positively influences all other factors. This makes it rather central to the development of judgement-making and might understandably cast uncertainty on whether it is reasonable to expect novices to develop this area of expertise. However, students and novice teachers are constantly accruing experience through their practicum and early career practice and the potential of this time should not be underestimated. Three elements appear regularly in the literature and seem important to the development of teacher judgement, even in the absence of lengthy experience: first, appropriate classroom conditions, including trust, openness to learning from mistakes and permission to judge (Meijer et al, 2011; Beck and Kosnik, 2002; Ulvik and Smith, 2011); second, expert mentoring (Harrison et al, 2005; Hargreaves and Fullan, 2012); and third, reflection (Schön, 1991; Pollard, 2008; Helleve et al, 2021). Evidence suggests that when these elements are present, even limited exposure to classroom teaching can become a fertile ground for the development of judgements 1 and 2.

IN A **NUTSHELL**

This chapter has presented a range of perspectives on teacher judgement and argued that it should not simply be left to experienced teachers. The development of classroom judgement is very much a concern for pre-service and novice teachers, and consequently, those who educate and mentor them. I have asserted that the key reason that judgement is an integral aspect of teaching is because schools and classrooms, and the teaching and learning processes within them, are complex. Human judgement is an inevitable requirement within indeterminate human systems. I have divided teacher judgements into two types (judgements 1 and 2) and presented a simple model to illustrate factors which contribute to teachers' use of judgement 2. Developments of this model appear in later chapters to help explain more specifically how the different factors influence one another, while influencing a teacher's judgements. There is no question that judgement is one of the most complex skills teachers are required to develop, not least because it is extremely challenging to sum up precisely what it looks like and from where it emerges. For the novice teacher, the challenge is greater still since some of the ways it develops lie beyond conscious control. Even those factors which can be deliberately worked on require demanding and time-consuming applications of structured reflection. However, the rewards of investing in accelerating judgement development are as significant for teachers as they are for the pupils they teach.

REFLECTIONS ON **CRITICAL ISSUES**

- Professional judgement is central to teaching and learning because schools and classrooms are dynamic, complex environments.
- Teaching demands judgement and developing professional judgement should be a priority for pre-service and novices teachers.
- Therefore, the development of practices and conditions associated with making judgements should be nurtured and encouraged in teacher education.
- Professional judgements can be thought of in two interdependent but distinct (at least in time and place) categories: before/after the moment (judgement 1) and in-the-moment judgements (judgement 2).
- Experience plays a central role in judgement development; however, we cannot assume capacities will just appear; effective teaching and mentoring are important.
- Lack of professional capital and the licence to decide in the classroom are challenges for pre-service and, to a lesser extent, for novice teachers. There is no easy fix for this, particularly in the case of pre-service teachers; however, teacher educators and mentors can help novices make the most of the experience they have.

CHAPTER 3 | EXPLORING THE COMPLEXITIES OF CLASSROOM TEACHING

CRITICAL ISSUES

- *Can we capture the complex nature of classroom teaching and learning?*
- *Distinguishing between the simple, the complicated and the complex.*
- *How do complexity and judgement relate?*
- *What are the consequences of complexity?*
- *What can we expect from pre-service and novice teachers?*

Introduction

Chapter 2 alluded to a relationship between the complexities of the classroom teaching and professional judgements, types 1 and 2. This chapter builds on this by exploring that relationship in more detail, asking what complexity means in the context of school classrooms, how the various classroom actors, their activities and interactions create complex phenomena, and how early career and soon-to-be teachers can respond to it. Like many domains of human activity, teaching and learning have an indeterminate quality about them; they are not fixed, their outcomes cannot be predicted with absolute certainty and their processes are to varying degrees dynamic, rather than inert. Shulman (2004, p 504) describes teaching, somewhat dramatically, as '*perhaps the most complex, most challenging, and most demanding, subtle, nuanced and frightening activity that our species ever invented*'. This may be something of an over-statement; however, anyone who has ever tried to teach anything to a group of learners for a sustained period will appreciate precisely what Shulman is getting at. Teaching is riddled with uncertainty and as suggested in the previous chapter, where events and their outcomes unfold in uncertain ways, there are limits on how effective prescribed, predetermined responses can be; this is where judgement comes into its own.

Capturing the complexity of classroom teaching and learning

Awareness of the complexities of classroom teaching and learning is widespread among teachers, teacher educators and educational researchers and, perhaps not surprisingly, references to complexity and the characteristics which produce it appear quite regularly in education literature. In policy, media and wider public perceptions, however, portrayals of learning and its relationship to teaching remain stubbornly simplistic and mechanistic. In what we might call the popular view of teaching and learning, the former produces the latter in something akin to a transmission and absorption, input–output process. Examples of this in education policy are found in the TS for England and Wales (DfE, 2011) and tessellating policies of national testing, league tables and school inspection which, despite reforms over several decades, still tend to present learning as a well-formed, well-understood problem and teaching as a set of clear, easily implementable solutions. Naturally, this routinising of teaching and of perceptions of teaching (see Kirk, 2020; Pattinson, 2020; Adams, 2019; BBC, 2019 for examples in television and print media) perpetuates an inauthentic version of teaching and learning by skimming over their complexities, or ignoring them altogether. Of course, in a way, teaching does cause learning to occur, and high-quality teaching probably strengthens that causal relationship. However, as others have also pointed out, the relationship is not a mechanistic one. Since learning is not a guaranteed product of teaching, at least not at the pace or in the manner we might like, it would be more accurate to say that teaching creates the conditions in which learning can emerge. As Derrida (1988, p 119) pointed out,

One shouldn't complicate things for the pleasure of complicating, but one should also never simplify or pretend to be sure of such simplicity where there is none. If things were simple, word would have gotten around...

It is fair to say that if learning mechanistically followed teaching, we would all know about it by now! Unfortunately, the pace, manner and even emergence of learning during or following a given episode of teaching cannot be guaranteed and discourse which portrays teaching and learning this way is simply inaccurate. Mencken (cited in Ciotti, 1983, p 37) puts it in even more forthright terms: '*For every complex problem, there is a solution that is simple, obvious, and wrong*'.

Let us pause here and look at some descriptions of classroom teaching and learning which emphasise their complexity. Davis and Sumara (2006, p 18) view classrooms as systems which adapt and learn through the interactions of their internal agents, principally pupils and teachers. They assert the following.

One cannot reliably predict how a student or a classroom collective will act based on responses in an earlier lesson, or sometimes a few minutes previous. In other words, strict predictability and reliability of results are unreasonable criteria when dealing with systems that learn.

One implication of this somewhat bold statement is that teachers should not presume they will always get the same outcomes from the same inputs, something most teachers will have little difficulty agreeing with I suspect. Another implication I would push back against, however, is that experience is not a reliable reference point for future decision making. Classrooms certainly are dynamic environments but not to the extent that prior experiences cannot inform judgement. Teachers must be open-minded and adaptable, but the past is definitely a useful tool when navigating the present and future. Also focusing on the idea that strict predictability is not a characteristic of classroom teaching and learning, Doll (1993, pp 101–2) posits that learning may be anticipated, but not predicted.

The teaching-learning frame switches from a cause-effect one where learning is either a direct result of teaching or teaching is at least in a superior-inferior relationship with learning. The switch is to a mode where teaching becomes ancillary to learning [...] The teaching role here is ancillary, not causative.

The concept of learning being *attached* to teaching is similar to the often-cited idea that teaching facilitates learning. Facilitating involves creating conditions in which something can happen and is qualitatively different from the idea of causing. Burns and Knox (2011, p 8) explain the unpredictability of classroom outcomes in the following way:

In many classrooms, the outcome of development over time cannot be predicted [...] because the variables that interact keep changing over time.

Erickson (1996, p 33) explains the variables Burns and Knox allude to in the quotation above are teachers and pupils.

Teachers and students interact in classrooms, they construct an ecology of social, cognitive relations in which influence between any and all parties is mutual, simultaneous and continuous.

Hardman (2010) suggests that the complexity of school classrooms is evident in the fact that, thus far, accurate descriptions of how they function, and in my view how learning occurs in particular, have eluded scholars and researchers. For Hardman (2010, p 8), this tacit nature of classroom learning highlights the importance of teacher professional judgement.

Classrooms are sensitive, dynamic and resistant to accurate description. This certainly seems to fit the experience of teachers and would be useful for new teachers to appreciate. Furthermore researchers and policy makers would do well to appreciate the limitations of their insights and allow teachers to operate using their professional experience and judgement.

I agree with Hardman's call for new teachers to recognise the complex dynamics of teaching and learning and would add that it befalls those of us involved in preparing and mentoring them to work out how best to achieve this. This is the principal motivation for writing this book. Also noteworthy is his implication that teachers must be allowed to exercise judgement. This fits with my own assertion in Chapter 2 that the acquisition of decisional capital relies in part on being permitted to judge.

The above quotations present ideas which help to explain why classrooms are such complex places and why planning for, steering and supporting classroom learning requires skilful judgement. First, there is the obvious characteristic that classrooms are unpredictable places and as emphasised in the previous chapter, when the outcomes of a given action cannot be reliably predicted, judgement becomes extremely useful. Second, that classrooms are systems and that their developments and outcomes depend not only on inputs, but also on the ecology of their interactions. To quote Haggis (2008, p 165) *'what emerges will depend on what interacts'*. In other words, what is learned by pupils is a function of more than simply input from teachers. What pupils do with that input, and how they do it, is also influential. Currently, a small but growing number of educational scholars and researchers are taking a complex systems-thinking approach to analysing classroom learning, considering not just the linear cause and effect of teaching and individual learning, but ways in which teachers influence pupils, pupils influence one another and how everyone influences and is influenced by the environment. I will say more about this and its use as a framework for understanding teaching and learning in the next section, but for now it is sufficient to understand complex systems-thinking as an approach which emphasises two key principles: self-organisation (that interactive systems organise themselves to some extent) and emergence (that new ideas may emerge from the bottom up). Finally, classroom systems do not remain static, they adapt and evolve over time. Any teacher reading this will attest to the fact that their classrooms do not feel the same halfway through the school year as they did at the start of the year, or that by the end of the year they feel quite different than they did at the midpoint. Pupils learn and are changed by their own and others' learning, relationships develop due to a wealth of shared experiences and teachers themselves are changed, meaning that they are not exactly the people they were at the beginning of the school year. This constant movement of the system demands that teachers constantly reflect upon, evaluate, update and adapt their responses to classroom events, and I would argue judgement is at the heart of these processes.

The simple, the complicated and the complex

To further our appreciation of the complexity of classrooms, it is useful to pause momentarily and consider exactly what complexity is and is not, and the implications of ascribing it to teaching and learning processes. Complex systems-thinking offers some useful perspectives from which teachers can reflect on and examine classroom teaching and learning, though this comes with a health warning. In complex systems, the individual units do not matter, only the aggregate patterns of behaviour across the whole system matter; the unit of analysis is the system, not the individuals within it. The limitations of this position when applied to education are self-evident; nevertheless, I believe a complex system view of classroom teaching and learning can be useful. Let us begin by exploring what we mean by complex, by differentiating it from the associated concepts, simple and complicated.

Simple systems

Cause and effect in simple systems is linear and mechanistic, which means that the outputs of the system are predictable products of the inputs, much like a manufacturing production line. If the workers at every point on the assembly line in a Ford factory input the correct parts and processes one can reliably predict that as components are fitted the assemblage will increasingly resemble a car and the eventual output of the system will be the desired Ford model. Simplicity, in this sense, is not a judgement about the ease or difficulty of the assembly (I am quite sure workers on a car assembly line would not appreciate the implication that their tasks are easy), rather it reflects the fact that the collective outcome of each task is known in advance. If any worker deviates from their prescribed role, the output will not be the desired model and is unlikely to function adequately. It is not difficult to make the case that teaching and learning do not bear much resemblance to simple systems. Although they do involve repeated processes and routines, the inputs of these are subject to a range of influences which make their outputs at least partly unpredictable.

Complicated systems

While the systems for assembling new cars may be simple and linear, the cars themselves are complicated machines. From a systems-thinking perspective, complicated refers to the intricacy of the system. To stay with the car analogy for now, car engines (particularly modern computerised ones) are inordinately complicated. They have many moving parts which interact with one another in multiple ways simultaneously. The action of one element has a knock-on effect on the elements with which it interacts creating a system within which a malfunction in any one element will be felt across the system. It is difficult for all but the most highly trained individuals to understand the effects of every cause since (unlike a production line) when the engine is running there is no beginning or end point. This is a complicated system, and there are parallels here with classroom teaching and learning, which also has no definite start or end point but continuously builds on and makes use of prior experiences. There are many moving parts at work in a typical classroom including teachers, pupils and support staff, the curriculum, the timetable, resources and the physical environment which mutually interact. These interactions certainly influence the system as a whole. However, what sets classrooms apart from complicated systems such as car engines has to do with their predictability. Although complicated systems have many interacting parts, they still behave with mechanistic predictability. Every component in a car engine has a single repeated job to do and, though cause and effect is networked across the system, rather than linear, the behaviour of each element remains consistent, like clockwork, and entirely predictable. Even when the engine has a fault, its predictability enables a mechanic to diagnose the problem and correct it. Classroom teaching and learning is quite different from this.

Complex systems

Similar to complicated systems, complex systems also have many moving, interacting parts. Unlike systems which are merely complicated, however, complex systems do not behave in mechanistic or predictable ways. They do not run like clockwork. Unlike a clock, a complex system is not closed off to outside influence; instead it is readily influenced by external elements which prevent its individual parts from always repeating the same behaviours and producing the same outcomes. Complex systems adapt over time meaning that they will not be exactly the same tomorrow, next week, month or year as they are today. A consequence of this is that actions which may have caused certain effects yesterday may cause different outcomes today. Such differences may be subtle, or even barely perceptible, or they may be pronounced and obvious, but either way managing a system which is constantly adapting requires constant adaptation on the part of the manager, in our case the teacher. Complexity educational researcher Mike Radford has used the analogy of clocks and clouds to explain how complicated and complex systems behave differently. According to Radford (2008), clock-like systems are deterministic in that they always behave in the same ways (much like clocks) and cloud-like systems are unpredictable and open; while their movements can be predicted with some degree of accuracy in the macro sense, the detail of their internal interactions is far from knowable (much like clouds). Radford asserts that all systems, mechanical or human, exist somewhere on a continuum between *clockish* and *cloudish*, but that if you zoom in closely enough even the most clockish systems are a bit cloudish and if you zoom out enough, even the most cloudish systems show signs of a clockish order. I have explored this assertion in relation to school classrooms in more detail elsewhere (see Knight, 2022a); however, for our purposes here, it is sufficient to say that classrooms tend to be a mixture of clockishness and cloudishness; complicated yes, but in some ways also complex. Table 3.1 shows some examples of processes common to classrooms and classroom teaching and learning which have complex characteristics.

Table 3.1 Examples of complex classroom characteristics.

Classroom feature or process	Complex nature	Implications of indeterminate outputs
Teacher modelling or explanation	Individual pupils process and assimilate information in different ways according to their prior learning and unique histories.	Learning occurs at different rates. Understandings about the same concepts differ. Teaching concepts in one way to all pupils on one occasion is not an option. Teachers require in-depth knowledge about individuals to predict and respond to learning needs.
Interactive group work	Pupil interactions may produce novel knowledge entities which emerge bottom-up from within the group rather than top-down from the teacher.	Unpredictable behaviours, questions, ideas, conclusions and actions may arise when pupils interact.
Lesson planning	No real starting or ending point. Outcomes from one iteration become the inputs for the next iterations, but since individual outcomes are not always predictable, the course of learning isn't either.	Lesson planning is only ever best guesswork. Thorough planning is important (especially for novice teachers) but should be viewed as a plotted course, not a script.

Table 3.1 (*Cont.*)

Classroom feature or process	Complex nature	Implications of indeterminate outputs
Relationships are pivotal	Subtle shifts in relationships between pupils or between pupils and teachers can have significant consequences for teaching and learning.	The relational/emotional climate in a classroom has consequences for almost everything which occurs. Pupils fall in and out of friendships, teachers manage the emotional temperature, and bridges are built and burned. The best planned lesson can be perturbed by relational/emotional factors.
Pupils operate between home and school environments	The classroom system is loosely bounded. Experiences beyond the classroom system influence what occurs within it, and vice versa. Teachers have limited control over external influences.	Pupil attitudes, motivations, interests, productivity and readiness to learn (among many other factors) are influenced by circumstances beyond the classroom. The classroom system is constantly subject to change from the outside.
Pupil autonomy	Handing autonomy to pupils introduces uncertainty and possibility into the classroom. Potential for significant learning and development coexists with potential for chaos.	Giving problem-solving and decision-making opportunities to pupils is important for social and intellectual development, but autonomy introduces uncertainty which teachers must manage.
Collision of ideas	Teachers and pupils ask and answer questions, share opinions, agree and disagree. Utterances can be unpredictable and inject novel insights and new directions into learning. When ideas collide pupils and teachers affect one another, and new knowledge entities may arise.	What pupils learn in group work scenarios may be more than, less than or different to that for which teachers planned. Where there is independence and interaction, outcomes may be unpredictable.

(continued)

Table 3.1 (*Cont.*)

Classroom feature or process	Complex nature	Implications of indeterminate outputs
Systems within systems	Classrooms comprise nested systems. Individuals, small groups and the whole class. Small groups learn because individuals within them learn, the class learns because the small groups learn and the school learns because the classes learn. Information flows within and across these nested systems.	Learning is not a linear transmission phenomenon, it won't appear on cue when a teacher wants it to and may surface unexpectedly among individuals and groups.

Common across the implications of each complex phenomenon in Table 3.1, and to all analysis of classrooms from a complex systems perspective, are uncertainty and unpredictability, and this is the essence of why professional judgement and its associated skills and dispositions are necessary ingredients for successful classroom teaching. The self-organising tendencies of classroom collectives and their proneness to bottom-up emergence means teachers must be able to respond to what is unforeseeable as well as what is planned for. Of course, teachers can control the effects of complexity in their classrooms to some extent through classroom and pupil organisation, task openness and behaviour management among other things, all of which are judgements. Biesta (2009, p 204) refers to such strategies as '*enabling constraints*' and describes their complexity decreasing effects as '*reducing the openness of the [classroom] system*', essentially making teaching and learning manageable. Likening complexity to Piaget's disequilibrium, Doll (1993, p 83) also advocates measures to keep it under control so that it does not '*turn into unbridled disruption*'. One common way in which teachers achieve this is through organisational structures. These tend to fall into three main categories: centralised, decentralised and distributed, and teachers may move between these multiple times in a single lesson. Figure 3.1 shows them in diagrammatic form.

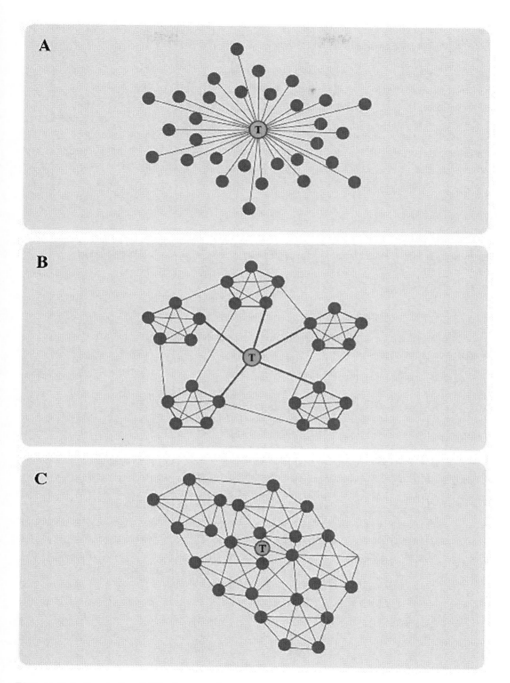

Figure 3.1 Centralised (A), decentralised (B) and distributed (C) classroom organisational structures (Knight, 2022b, adapted from Davis and Sumara, 2006)

In a centralised classroom structure (A), often used at beginnings and ends of lessons, the teacher addresses all pupils simultaneously and interactions are largely one way. The teacher is more active, and the pupils more passive. Complexity is most suppressed in this structure. In a decentralised structure (B), often used in the middle portions of lessons, pupils operate in small groups. The teacher may be in touch with each group, but the majority of interactions are between pupils. Complexity is less constrained than in a centralised approach. In a distributed structure (C), often occurring when a decentralised approach has outstayed its welcome, pupils have high degrees of autonomy to move and interact as they please. In this structure, complexity is least inhibited meaning that uncertainty and unpredictability are high. It is generally agreed that facilitating classroom learning demands all three structures at different points. The question is: how do pre-service and novice teachers make system-level judgements about when and how to shift between them?

What are the implications for pre-service and novice teachers?

My own research into classroom teaching and learning (Knight, 2022b) revealed a number of specific demands which complexity makes of teachers, some of which are worth exploring in the context of pre-service and novice teacher development. Developing competence in these areas can make system-level judgements about classroom organisation more fluent.

1. Comfort with knowledge and ideas moving between pupils

   It is not uncommon for pre-service and novice teachers to show reluctance to decentralise or distribute control in the classroom, largely because of concerns about classroom and behaviour management (see Hammond Stoughton, 2007 for a discussion of the evidence for this). However, engendering independence and encouraging autonomy and problem-solving skills are necessary prerequisites to a well-rounded education, and therefore this is an area where teachers simply must develop comfort and competence. Locating and capitalising on sweet-spot moments in classroom activity where circumstances are ripe for learning require that teachers be willing to relinquish centralised control, what Doll (1989, p 67) refers to rather wonderfully as 'more dancing and less marching'. While it is understandable that beginning teachers may feel tentative about it, becoming relaxed about loosening control, allowing greater autonomy and encouraging the movement of ideas between pupils are core elements of classroom teaching, and one which ought to form part of teacher education, at all phases.

2. Knowing how and judging when to centralise, decentralise or distribute classroom organisation in the interest of learning

Organisational structures typically shift through lessons and through a school day. Sometimes teachers hold the initiative and address the whole class in a didactic manner, sometimes they hand the initiative over to pupils organised into groups and sometimes they distribute initiative so that all pupils pursue their individual learning interests. The latter is particularly characteristic of early years pedagogy where principles such as individual uniqueness, independence and discovery are typically emphasised. Judging when (and knowing how) to transition between these organising principles is crucial from both classroom management and learning points of view. It involves sensitivity to emotional, cognitive and social aspects of classroom climate, picking up on soon-to-be learning (Knight, 2022b) and understanding about the particular power of each mode of organisation and how they may work together. As discussed in Chapter 2, these elements of disciplinary knowledge often remain tacit, but the work of teacher education and novice teacher mentoring includes bringing them into relief for the purposes of reflection.

3. Sensitivity to teachable moments

Teachers must become attuned to moments in which conditions are just right for learning to emerge and be able to exercise appropriate judgement to encourage its emergence. At the simpler end of the scale, this includes noticing when pupils hold misconceptions which can be challenged or tip of the tongue states (Dunlosky and Metcalfe, 2009) where understanding is imminent. At the more complex end, it may include noticing tipping points in understanding during small group or whole class interactions, observing when fruitful but partially formed ideas may be about to surface or appreciating how mistakes can be harnessed. As Doll (1993, p 67) puts it 'the teacher needs to be aware of more than one level of operation: the not-yet conscious, groping level as well as the performative'. Indicators of potential teachable moments are often subtle and as much about awareness of social/emotional factors, body language, attitudes, motivation or engagement. Judging how to respond in such situations, including tailoring responses to individuals, scaffolding without over-scaffolding, deciding what is or is not possible in a given time frame and monitoring impact on the wider class collective is important. However, these are not skills and dispositions one can simply switch on, they require teaching and mentoring. Teachers typically feel their way in such circumstances; however, there are some underpinning principles which can help them capitalise on teachable moments which we will address in Chapter 4.

4. Understanding learning as a process (or series of processes), not an event

Building on the concept of soon-to-be learning from point 2 and teachable moments from point 3, classroom complexity means that learning does not necessarily appear on cue or in neat packages based on stated learning objectives. Learning itself is a somewhat unpredictable process, not an event. Like all complex phenomenon, it has no discernible start or end point, instead it is continuous and does not progress upwards at a steady pace or trajectory. In classrooms, this means teachers have their work cut-out for, as Ollerton (2014, p 43) puts it, *'Learning is messy'*. Part of the disciplinary knowledge toolkit of a teacher is an appreciation of this fact, though in my experience it is rarely emphasised as clearly or as often as it ought to be.

What does this mean for judgement 1?

As explained in Chapter 2, I have categorised teacher judgements into two broad types (see Figure 1.1 on page 2) and aligned them roughly with Schön's (1987) two forms of reflection. Judgement 1 involves decisions a teacher might make about their teaching and pupils' learning while removed from the actual act of teaching. These decisions involve reflection *on* previous action. Judgement 2 consists of in-the-moment judgements about teaching and learning. Such judgements are likely to be the consequences of reflection *in* action. The case study featuring pre-service teacher Luke and its follow-up discussion in Chapter 2 provides some useful illustrations of the ways classroom complexity creates the need for judgement 2. Here I would like to explore its implications for judgement 1 (see Figure 4.1 in the following chapter).

Complexity and judgement 1

When teachers reflect on previous actions and their consequences while removed from the teaching moment, there is greater potential for understanding the bigger picture. Unlike category 2 judgements which tend to involve making small adjustments in situ which may only alter the course of the lesson or activity in question, category 1 judgements will often affect teaching and learning over longer periods. The consequences of category 1 judgements may be felt over multiple lessons, weeks or semesters. Judgement 1 often enables teachers to view the classroom, curriculum content and pupil learning from a systems perspective, to evaluate how successful processes and routines are operating in relation to their aims and to diagnose and problematise system weaknesses. These could include, for example, realisations that their usual lesson structure may be becoming monotonous and needs more variety, that the seating plan is creating some difficulties or that a concept or topic needs revisiting. Understanding and thinking about the classroom as a complex system and teaching and learning a complex phenomenon can help teachers to appreciate the possible consequences of their decisions and actions, intended or otherwise. It can also help them to see failures (eg difficulties pitching activities appropriately, apparent lack of learning, disruptive behaviours) as to some extent inevitable, but also as problems with multiple causes requiring multiple solutions. This is a crucial point. An important characteristic revealed by a complex systems-thinking approach to the classroom is that effects rarely have single causes; therefore, when identifying effects in the classroom which are not conducive to productivity and learning, a sensible teacher response would be to consider the range of possible contributing factors. This short case study offers an everyday example.

CASE **STUDY**

Olivia, an early career teacher in her second term since qualifying, reflects on her observation that the collaborative group-work elements of her lessons are characterised by low productivity, time-wasting, peer conflict and regular teacher interventions. Understanding the importance of handing autonomy and independence to pupils and knowing from her observations of more experienced colleagues that group work can be a useful way of managing this, she is keen to find ways of making interactive group work more effective in her lessons.

A complex systems-thinking approach could be very helpful for Olivia in this situation because it will lead her to consider multiple causes for the difficulties she has observed, including ways she may be inadvertently contributing to them; after all, teachers are complicit in the system. Understanding the classroom as a system containing smaller systems (including small groups) may encourage her to consider how teaching and learning at whole class and individual levels may be impacting on learning at small group level. Knowing that the classroom system is open to outside influence, she may consider ways in which factors from pupils' home lives or from the wider school community may be contributing to the issue or could be harnessed to help solve it. Understanding that greater pupil autonomy and higher density of interactions increase classroom complexity may prompt her to consider making groups smaller, making tasks less open or making group work periods shorter in duration. Knowing that the classroom system comprises individual pupils with unique personalities, personal histories and social status may cause her to reconsider the composition of pupil groupings. These are all examples of system-level judgement calls enabled by the more detached vantage point of judgement 1. These big picture judgements can help teachers to adapt the structural (or systemic) organisation and behaviours of the system in the interests of learning.

IN A **NUTSHELL**

This chapter has explored in more detail the broad assertion from Chapter 2 that the reason judgement is so pivotal to classroom teaching is because classrooms and the teaching and learning within them are complex. If classroom dynamics, interactions, content and learning only changed in response to teachers' design, then the business of teaching would be far more straightforward and require far less judgement; predetermined structures and plans would do the job quite nicely. It is because classrooms are to some extent self-organising systems, with minds of their own we might say, that judgement is integral to successful teaching. I have drawn on elements of complex systems-thinking to illustrate ways in which classroom complexity reveals itself day to day and suggested that taking a systems approach to evaluating teaching and learning processes, and understanding the classroom itself as a system, can aid professional development and provide useful prompts for type 2 judgements. If novice teachers can be supported to get judgements 1 and 2 functioning in conjunction with one another, which I argue is the beating heart of their professionalism, then classroom complexity need not be a daunting, or even overwhelming, prospect. A useful ambition for pre-service and new teachers might be to:

1. understand that classroom systems have some self-organising properties;

2. judge, plan for and implement developments at system level over time (judgement 1).

REFLECTIONS ON **CRITICAL ISSUES**

- Capturing precisely the ways in which classroom teaching and learning are complex is difficult and beyond the scope of this book. However, we can explain why teaching does not simply produce learning in a mechanistic manner using examples from theory and practice.

- Accepting that complexity is an inevitable consequence of the teaching and learning endeavour, the task for teachers is to develop strategies for navigating and managing it in the interest of pupil learning; what I refer to as 'managed complexity'.

- Judgement seems to be a key tool for teachers faced with the unpredictability of a complex environment like a classroom and complex phenomena like teaching and learning.

- Pre-service and novice teachers should be forgiven for feeling daunted by the demands which complexity makes. However, it seems reasonable to expect that with sound mentoring they can develop approaches and confidence to begin to manage complexity in their classrooms.

CRITICAL **ISSUES**

- *If judgement is central to teaching, how can it be nurtured?*
- *If judgement relies on experience, what value can university-based teacher education bring?*
- *How do judgements about specific critical incidents and classroom system-level events intersect to produce effective judgement?*
- *Should university-based teacher educators be doing more to encourage professional judgement?*
- *What is required of teacher educators and school-based mentors?*

Introduction

The preceding chapters have explored some ways of understanding what professional judgement is, ways it can reveal itself in teaching and learning and why it is central to teaching. In this chapter, we build on this by discussing how teacher judgement can be nurtured. Having already established that professional judgement draws on both practical experience and disciplinary knowledge (among other things), our attention here is focused on both university-based teacher education and school-based mentoring. This includes the development and application of theoretical and practical knowledge which, as discussed in Chapter 1, can be useful bedfellows when developing the skills of effective judgement. The key question this chapter aims to address is how can novice teachers be supported to grow into expert judges of classroom teaching and learning situations?

The chapter is organised around the two broad and overlapping categories of judgements introduced in Chapter 1 and discussed in Chapters 2 and 3. For the benefit of readers who have begun reading from this chapter, in brief, these categories are:

Judgement 1, which involves looking ahead and planning for future action, drawing on prior events and taking account of a range of known (and unknown) complexities to make system-level (global) adjustments to classroom practice;

Judgement 2, which involves improvising in situ to adjust the course of classroom action in pursuit of optimal conditions for teaching and learning.

Taking them in turn, I discuss ways in which university-based teacher education and school-based mentoring can nurture their development by encouraging novices to (1) draw on sources of knowledge and (2) develop useful habits of mind. There are considerable areas of crossover between factors which enable these two categories of judgements, including reflection, different types of knowledge and experience for example; however, in this chapter, I discuss them separately for ease and clarity. Having already explored the anatomy of category 2 judgements in some length in Chapter 2, I spend longer on category 1 judgements.

What can teacher educators and early career mentors do?

Appreciating that guiding soon-to-be and novice teachers relies on thoughtful collaboration between university and school-based colleagues, it is worthwhile to consider some of the key contributions both can make to the development of professional judgement. We will return to this important question throughout the chapter, but to begin with, I wish to emphasise two important points about the ways teaching as a profession and judgement as a skillset could be usefully conceptualised. Without these, it is difficult to envisage a shift from the tacit to the explicit development of professional judgement. Teacher educators and early career mentors should:

» understand and communicate the complexities of teaching. This is a point discussed by Burn et al (2015, p 14) in their excellent book about school-based teacher education, who state:

If we are to support beginners effectively, we first need to acknowledge just how complex the task of teaching is. If we do not adequately recognise the challenges involved [...] then we will fail to prepare our trainees for the shock of that discovery.

As I have previously said, anyone who has ever been a classroom teacher implicitly understands this. However, developing an explicit understanding of this would enable teacher educators to articulate and explore the issue productively. Understanding and explaining that teaching is full of challenges is one thing, but being able to model, illustrate and discuss what this complexity looks like and ways of navigating it would be considerably more helpful. Not only would this prepare novices for the realities of the role, it would also help to centre judgement as a core teacher skill.

» champion teacher judgement and decision making as a core skillset. Judgement has a habit of lurking in the background during teacher education and school-based mentoring, alluded to but rarely articulated or explored. Actual teacher decisions and judgements may be discussed frequently, though in my experience the central roles they play in teaching and learning are emphasised and explored less often, as are the processes which led to actual decisions. A central theme of this book is that good professional judgement *is* good teaching and following on from this, if teacher educators and school mentors are to be instrumental in shaping good teachers, they must explicitly teach about, encourage, prioritise and champion its development.

Teacher educators and mentors who are convinced of the value of these two points will find there are a few easy wins when incorporating them into their teaching and mentoring. When delivering lectures or seminars teacher educators could, for example:

» speak explicitly about the complex nature of teaching;

» use the language of professional judgement, for example decision making, choosing, selecting, adjusting, evaluating, adapting. If judgement is at the heart of teaching (as I have argued in previous chapters), then the language of judgement should permeate teacher education;

» highlight instances in which judgement is routinely required, for example when planning for learning, giving feedback on pupils' work, selecting resources or considering lesson pace;

» highlight the interconnectedness of teaching and learning across the curriculum. This is particularly relevant to early years and primary phases where multiple curriculum subjects are taught by the same teacher in the same space;

» emphasise that classroom events and processes are interconnected and therefore decisions made about one aspect of practice, for example adjusting seating arrangements or resources, will have foreseen and unforeseen knock-on effects to other aspects;

» emphasise the context-sensitive nature of teaching and learning, especially the idea that the particular pupils in a given classroom will respond in unique ways and create *'uniquely configured events'* (Clark and Yinger, 1987, p 18) through their interactions;

» explore the nexus of theory and practice thoroughly.

For school-based and early career mentors it might involve:

» creating safe spaces within classroom practice for the rehearsal of judgements;

» allowing trainees and novices to rehearse and reflect in low-stakes contexts;

» discussing with novices the importance of developing an evaluative internal monologue while *in* the action of teaching;

» allocating dedicated time for novices to reflect *on* action, including reflecting on their reflections (metacognitive reflection);

» using the language of judgement (see above);

» ensuring teaching tasks are well matched to a novice's current capability so that they experience some complexity and are required to make judgements, but without being overwhelmed.

The following sections explore approaches which teacher educators and early career mentors might adopt to explicitly teach, and hopefully accelerate the development of, professional judgement skills in novice teachers navigating the complexities of the classroom. It begins with a focus on category 1 judgement.

The development of judgement 1: encouraging system-level reflections on classroom teaching and learning

In Chapter 3, I argued for the value of reflecting on teaching and learning from a zoomed-out, system-level perspective. Only category 1 judgements involve the wider frame of reference needed to see the *big picture* and pull levers necessary to make structural changes to the ways a classroom system behaves. This is not to say that judgement 1 cannot also be a productive source of reflections about micro incidents and events in teaching and learning, but bigger picture judgements can only be made from the removed vantage point of category 1 judgement; and herein lies its real power. This is evident in the experience, common to all teachers, of ideas occurring to them spontaneously when away from the classroom. In a study by Dunn and Shriner (1999, p 641), one teacher reported that *'ideas come to me at the craziest times, like my driving. "Oh, it would be great to do that!"'* Another reported that ideas frequently emerged when walking the dog. Distance from the act of teaching, whether in or out of school, seems to unlock insights which the moment of teaching cannot. In this section, we will look at ways novice teachers can be encouraged to develop the mindset and skillset for judgement 1.

An obvious place to start is with the value of developing system-level habits of mind, which means reflecting on and reasoning about classroom teaching and learning holistically. In a general sense, a system is just a collection of parts connected by some form of interaction. Ndaruhutse et al (2019, p 13) explain it as follows:

a set of components that work together as a whole to achieve a common objective. A system is greater than the sum of its constituent components because the relationship between the different components adds value to the system.

Systems-thinking therefore prioritises the whole over those constituent parts by focusing on the ways they interact and influence one another, a central tenet being that the system cannot be reduced to its basic elements (Arnold and Wade, 2015). Understanding a system requires cognisance of how its internal elements interact and an eye for what emerges as a result. Barry Richmond, widely considered as the originator of systems-thinking, described it in the following way:

The systems thinking vantage point is best characterized by the term bifocal. That is, people employing systems thinking position themselves so that they can see both the forest and the trees (one eye on each).

(Richmond, 1994, pp 139–40)

In this sense, a teacher taking a systems-thinking reflective approach sees both the micro and the macro pictures and reasons about how they relate. In terms of developing judgement 1, this might mean helping trainees and novices to appreciate the following.

» Systems, routines and procedures are interconnected; therefore, adjustments in one area are likely to involve adjustments to multiple areas. When intervening to address a concern, teachers should have their eyes on the possible range of consequences which might follow from their intervention. Some might be desirable, others less so. For example, it is common (and understandable) for teachers to instinctively intervene when pupils go off-task; however, studies have shown that, somewhat unintuitively, off-task talk among pupils can play important roles in support of learning (Langer-Osuna, 2018; Dyson, 1987). In this case, a possible consequence of intervening may be that learning suffers. A teacher might understandably want to put a stop to such talk during lessons but should be helped to realise that some valuable opportunities may be lost when doing so. This is a judgement call, but only by adopting a systems-thinking approach are teachers likely to make such judgements successfully.

» Classrooms as teaching and learning entities are dynamic, not inert. They adapt over time. Experienced teachers will attest to the fact that a single strategy rarely has the same effect throughout an entire school year, or even that what was successful yesterday might not be today. This can be particularly true when managing classroom behaviour. Pupils become habituated to routines and respond differently to them over time. This dynamism has been highlighted by many researchers but, as Johnson (2016) points out, is often excluded from discussions about improving teaching and learning. The slightly removed vantage point of judgement 1 offers useful opportunities for reflecting on how the classroom system may be changing and how teachers' responses may have to adapt in light of this.

» Pupil learning – individual, group or whole class – is a function of more than just a teacher's input. This principle is central to assertions that teaching and learning are not mechanistically linked (see Chapters 2 and 3 for more on this), and that teachers should therefore not expect *all* pupils to have mastered a given learning objective at the end of a given lesson, even when grouped or streamed with similarly capable peers. Teachers are managers of a wide range of factors, not least the uniqueness of the pupil collective in front of them. This is not to dismiss the usefulness of direct teacher input (far from it), but to emphasise that this forms part of the system-level organisation for which a teacher is responsible and upon which learning depends. I like the way Dalke et al (2007, p 6) put it:

The teacher's distinctive role is to create the kind of rich environment within which productive organisations can emerge from the interactions of all participants.

This helps explain why the same lesson being taught by the same teacher to two parallel classes can produce such different results. Despite their many shared similarities (age, location, broad developmental trajectories), every class of pupils is unique. It is useful for novices to consider the range of factors which, in addition to their teaching, influence how and to what extent pupils make progress.

» Teachers themselves are constantly influencing the way the classroom system behaves, consciously and unconsciously. Sullivan (2009, p 185) refers to teachers as the '*keystone species*' in the ecology of a classroom due to the sway they hold over events and behaviours. He describes them as *influencing*, while not necessarily *determining*, what transpires. In many ways, this goes without saying. However, as Burns and Knox (2011) show, less predictable or expected teacher influences (eg from personality, personal interests, prior education or just having a bad day) can also impact what transpires in lessons, in more subtle ways. This helps explain why the same lesson taught by two different teachers in parallel classes can also produce such different results.

» Collective habits, behaviours, routines and sub-cultures emerge from the bottom-up. These may be conducive or detrimental (or both) to learning. As all pre-service and novice teachers find out upon entering classrooms, there is a lot more going on than simply teacher input, pupil activity and pupil learning. These key things are mediated by a multitude of less visible forces and factors, most of which emerge from within the complex interactions of the pupils themselves. Class mood (Canovi et al, 2019), social status jostling (Hendrickx et al, 2017; Acquah et al, 2014), and changing pupil friendships (Blatchford et al, 2015), for example all exert considerable influence over teachers' efforts to inspire, motivate, challenge and engender productivity and learning in their pupils.

» The complexity of a classroom system increases as density of pupil interaction increases. Returning to this point from Chapter 3 and building on the assertion about teacher influence above, it is useful for pre-service and novice teachers to understand that while teachers are by no means puppeteers (a point which is central to the aims and arguments of this book), they can (and should) manage the complexity of the classroom system. An effective means of achieving this is by moving strategically between centralised, decentralised and distributed organisational structures (see Chapter 3) to regulate classroom complexity in the interests of curriculum learning and avoiding all-out havoc. Generally speaking, the greater the density of pupil interactions, the greater the complexity.

The above points are all examples of system-level reasoning we can associate with category 1 judgements. In Chapter 2, I presented a model for thinking about how category 2 judgements are formed. This included factors relating to permission and capacity to judge, as well as sources of knowledge and inspiration for judgements. Figure 4.1 models category 1 judgement in a similar way by depicting things which influence judgements made *on* action. In order to capitalise on the vantage point which judgement 1 offers, teacher educators and classroom mentors could encourage novice teachers to reflect on these factors.

JUDGEMENT 1

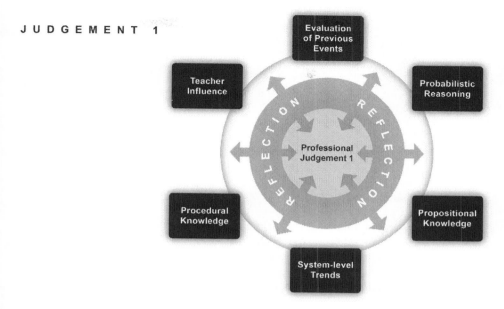

Figure 4.1 Factors contributing to category 1 professional judgements

Evaluation of previous events

Evaluative reflection on prior events, actions, consequences and outcomes plays a key role in planning for future action. According to Schön (1987), this includes metacognitive reflections on our reflections *in* action, which means that it is important for novice teachers not only to reflect on past events, but also to reflect on their in-the-moment reflections at the time. In doing so, the novice is really asking: '*What were the salient events, what were my in-situ reflections, what judgements and actions resulted from them and what were the consequences?*' Teachers frequently make use of hunches and instincts formed in the moment and turn these into category 1 judgements once removed from the moment. These layers of reflection are central to forming judgements about future system-level decision making. They also provide the basis for a teacher's self-evaluation of their professional judgement, and are key to answering questions like '*how useful and productive are my judgements?*' Being able to articulate such self-evaluations, verbally or in writing, is a crucial part of learning to judge.

Probabilistic reasoning

Reflecting evaluatively about prior events enables teachers to form judgements about future actions by reasoning about the decisions and actions which are most likely to produce desired effects. If encouraged to engage in systems-thinking about classroom teaching and learning, it also enables them to consider unexpected or possible unwanted consequences of these actions. While in judgement 2 they may reason in a quick and somewhat fuzzy or intuitive way about such things, judgement 1 facilitates a slower, more considered approach to plotting decisions about the best ways forward. Probabilistic reasoning is an essential component when working in and with uncertain systems which, as I have argued, classrooms certainly seem to be. To successfully judge the best course for future action, the pre-service or novice teacher should be encouraged to understand prior events and their multiple consequences in some detail, isolating and linking causes and effects for the outcomes they observe. In-school mentoring, in particular, plays a key role in this because of its proximity to actual teaching.

System-level trends

Conceptualising and reflecting on classroom teaching and learning as a system will enable novices to notice trends in the ways the system is changing over time and respond to these during moments of reflection. Without a system-level view, it is easy to become locked into zoomed-in thinking about individual incidents and fail to appreciate how these might all connect together. The ability to switch between zoomed-in and zoomed-out thinking about the classroom (seeing both the woods and the trees) can positively influence judgement 1 and the decisions which flow from it. A teacher's ability to interpret system-level trends in their classrooms is unlocked by reflections on experiences of classroom teaching. Because classroom systems, unlike some other systems, are purpose-driven, the task here is to draw on prior experiences to judge how successfully trends in behaviours, efficiencies, relationships, organisations or pupil attitudes are operating in the interest of that purpose, pupil learning. This means teachers having clarity about intended aims, broad and specific, and understanding which aspects of the system (resources, timetabling, physical space, teacher input for example) may need to be tweaked to achieve them. Wong and Wong (2014) refer to this as being a 'systems-orientated teacher'.

Teacher influence

System-level thinking about classroom events, processes and outcomes demands that teachers reflect on their own influence on those events, processes and outcomes. This includes not only the *intended* influence of their actions and interventions, but also inevitable *unintended* results. Reasoning about the law of unintended consequences is always challenging, particularly for novices since these sorts of judgements do tend to draw considerably on past experiences. However, it is a very useful habit of mind for training and new teachers to develop because it provides a very useful template for the sort of thinking which will eventually help them to weigh up the pros and cons of possible future actions. Shulman (2004, p 263) urges teachers to consider the unintended consequences of their actions, referring (again somewhat dramatically) to any decision or intervention as potentially '*two-edged swords, blessings dipped in acid for teachers*'. Key questions a novice might ask when reasoning about a future action include the following.

> » What is the intended outcome of action A?

> » How significant might the outcome be?

» Are there any possible unintended outcomes from Action A?

» Can these be avoided or are they worth risking for the benefits of Action A?

A brief case study puts this into a more real context.

CASE **STUDY**

Teacher reflections at the end of the school day

Priya, an early career teacher, is reviewing pupils' work after school, giving feedback advice and reflecting on the Year 10 English lesson she taught during the last period of the day. In this lesson, pupils were challenged to write about the motivations of characters in a certain scene from the examination set text. She notices persistent errors in the work produced by pupils from the two tables at the rear of the classroom which appears to have become a trend over recent weeks. Most of these pupils have written about different characters from different scenes. The work itself is not bad, but a pattern of misunderstanding expectations for tasks seems to be forming for these groups over multiple lessons.

In weighing up how to respond, Priya considers the pros and cons of asking the pupils to redo the task using the correct characters. Her initial instinct is to do just that. She knows it is quite likely that questions about character motivation in the exam will be focused on the characters she selected and that having worked on those characters will be helpful. She isn't sure how the error happened but knowing that these particular pupils are easily distracted and tend to copy one another, she also feels that a mistake like this ought to be corrected. Reflecting on the fact that this is something of a trend for these pupils, she also feels the need to make some adjustments to the way she introduces tasks and maybe the class seating plan. On the other hand, these are not particularly motivated pupils and what they have produced took each of them a lot of effort. Telling them tomorrow that they all need to redo it will not go without complaint and likely disruption. If she does insist they redo the work, these two tables will also then be out of sync with the activities set for the rest of the class. This in turn is likely to have a disruptive effect on others. This is a judgement call.

Priya is beginning to think about the possible consequences which may follow from her decisions. Ultimately, she made a judgement call (she made them do it again) and made the best of the unintended consequences of this. Through reflection with her early career mentor, she also learned some valuable lessons which can be applied to future judgements. This included the importance of ensuring that all pupils understand task expectations in advance. Effective mentoring in situations like this can be invaluable for early career teachers, not because a mentor should tell an early career teacher what to do, but because a mentor can play a crucial role in helping structure their thinking when faced with similar dilemmas.

Propositional and procedural knowledge

Judging the best course of action always involves drawing on multiple sources of knowledge; this is part of the complexity of teaching. However, when faced with a dilemma or when reasoning to exercise judgement, we are often not conscious of these different sources; what surfaces as a mixture of propositional, procedural and experiential knowledge usually has its origins in the realm of the tacit. Or, as Davis (2004, p 130) puts it, *'Explicit knowledge is the mere surface of a knotted tangle of experience and interpretation'*. Although propositional and procedural knowledge make unique contributions to our reasoning when making judgements, they usually operate simultaneously and, in reality, when deciding on an intervention or action we draw on both without much dissection. While there is no special requirement for new teachers to disentangle or separately identify different knowledge sources when reflecting and planning, there is merit in developing and rehearsing the sort of mental habits which may enable them to get the most from such knowledge sources. At a basic level, this might mean asking questions like:

» how am I interpreting events?

» can I locate the issue/problem at hand?

» what can my knowledge of learning theory contribute to this dilemma?

» what about my subject knowledge?

» do I know or understand enough?

» what can my experiences of implementing practical changes contribute?

» what has/has not worked well previously?

An effective classroom mentor might encourage a trainee or new teacher to pose and reflect on such questions to help engender the sort of problem-solving habits conducive to expert judgement.

Key prompts from teacher educators and school-based mentors

Drawing on the model in Figure 4.1, the following section presents a range of key questions and prompts for reflection *on* action which teacher educators and school-based mentors could pose to encourage the sort of system-level habits of mind which lead to successful category 1 judgements.

Key questions and prompts from teacher educators

» What are the system-like features of classrooms?

» Why is it useful to conceptualise classroom events from both the critical incident *and* system behaviour perspectives?

» How does a classroom system interact with connected systems at other levels, for example the school, the community and pupils' homes?

» What are some of the consequences of the openness of a classroom system?

» Consider a range of system-level teacher interventions and how their effects might influence teaching and learning outcomes.

» What roles do you play in the classroom system? What can you influence directly/indirectly, comprehensively or only marginally?

» What factors, in addition to your teacher input, influence learning?

» What trends, routines or sub-cultures might emerge bottom-up? Should you intervene to capitalise on, or prevent them?

» How can propositional and procedural knowledge be integrated to refine your judgements?

Key questions and prompts from school-based mentors

» Can you identify the causes of the incident you are reflecting on? Were there multiple causes?

» What do your instincts suggest needs to be done?

» Have you considered the possible range of consequences of this or that action?

» How likely is this planned action to positively influence the situation?

» Can you reflect on your contributions to the challenges you experienced in that lesson? Were you creating part of the problem? How could you have done things differently?

» Why do you think that approach worked last week but really didn't work today?

» How useful were your in situ judgements and actions during those critical events in the lesson? Talk me through what led you to that decision.

The development of judgement 2: encouraging in-the-moment reasoning, problem-solving and action

Schön (1983) viewed expert practice as being more than simply the application of theory to practical situations. Rather, he saw effective practitioners as having the ability to discern and work with perplexing or ambiguous situations as they happen. A characteristic of such situations is that the issues to be resolved and the dilemmas they produce are rarely understood until they occur. Piet Hein captured this beautifully with the assertion that *'Art is solving problems that cannot be formulated before they have been solved. The shaping of the question is part of the answer'* (cited in Preble, 1973, p 14). This is the essence of reflection *in* action, and of category 2 judgements. Though judgement 2 is more the territory of the school-based mentor due to their proximity to the action of classroom teaching, there are several approaches which teacher educators can also take to encourage the development of these capabilities, by bringing the tacit knowledge of phronesis into consciousness. Suggestions for both teacher educators and school-based mentors are set out as follows.

Teacher educators might...

» Talk to pre-service teachers about the skills and dispositions which unlock and enable effective judgement in the moment. These include:

o having real-time internalised knowledge of the intended destination and planned routes for a lesson;

o monitoring of events;

o surveying the classroom, taking in contextual information;

o listening to pupils;

o evaluating processes and events through an internal monologue;

o asking regular situational appraisal questions;

o making best-fit decisions based on available information in the moment.

» Allocate time after school placements for trainees to reflect on these aspects of their practical experience. This might include:

o discussion about the purpose of lesson planning and how to manage uncertainties and unknowns which may arise during lessons;

o peer-to-peer review of example lessons and lesson plans, including discussion about how accurately the lesson(s) actually reflected the plan(s);

o reflection on how the demands for and of judgement 2 change in different situations, for example classroom lessons, outdoor physical education lessons, out of school excursions or break times.

» Create action plans to identify specific areas for conscious skill rehearsal on future practicum.

» Actively avoid what Shulman (2004, p 265) refers to as a '*monolithic image of "good practice"*' by conveying that effective practice varies, as do '*wise practitioners*'. Understanding that while there is much they can learn from the practice of experts and that some approaches are likely to be more effective than others, it is important for trainees to appreciate that '*effective*' can look quite different from one classroom to another; one teacher to another.

» Position subject knowledge development as integral to fluent in situ judgements.

School-based mentors might...

» Provide opportunities for trainees to observe expert teachers (themselves perhaps?), looking specifically for examples of category 2 judgements. Follow this up with out-loud reflections from the expert teacher about those critical incidents and judgement made.

» Watch recordings of lessons taught by trainees themselves, or experienced teachers, to analyse in situ judgements. Pause the recording regularly to pick out and dissect critical incidents, including how trainees felt in the moment and how they feel now.

» Observe novices teaching, making a note of their in situ judgement calls for post-lesson reflection and discussion.

» Support novices to distinguish between judgements which can be made while planning and judgements which can only be made in the moment.

» Discuss novices' lesson plans, highlighting more indeterminate aspects of the lessons in order to pre-empt and consider possible judgement calls. This might look something like this:

Mentor: '*I see you're planning to take the pupils outside for this part of the lesson. Think ahead about possible unexpected things which might emerge in situ and what decisions you may be required to make*'.

Mentor: '*What will you need to be thinking about or sensitive to in order to make useful judgements in this part of the lesson?*'

» Remind novices to maintain a surveying eye and an evaluating mindset on the whole class throughout their lessons.

» Allocate time for reflection on judgements novices made during their teaching (metacognitive reflection).

» Resist the temptation (and it is a significant temptation) to regularly simply tell novices what to do. Instead, it is more powerful and productive for mentors to:

o talk and reason about their own thought processes;

o   elicit reasoning from novices;

o   offer explanations where they do give specific advice.

»   Create the conditions in which novices feel permitted to rehearse in situ judgements.

IN A **NUTSHELL**

This chapter has explored and presented a range of approaches which teacher educators and classroom mentors might take to encourage the development of professional judgement in pre-service and early career teachers. These suggested approaches involve:

- an appreciation of the complexities of classroom teaching;

- a commitment to positioning judgement as a core teacher skill;

- understanding classroom events from both critical incident and system perspectives;

- making explicit what often remains tacit so that novices can engage in deliberate and effortful reasoning and reflection about their developing skills;

- making time for reflection;

- eliciting insights from novices themselves more often than telling them what to do;

- encouraging habits of mind as much as specific skills.

REFLECTIONS ON **CRITICAL ISSUES**

- There is little doubt that judgement is central to successful teaching, and I have argued in this chapter that it ought to enjoy a more prominent position on teacher education programmes and in early career teacher frameworks.

- Since judgement is ever-present in teaching, nurturing it more deliberately should mean weaving it into every element of teacher education and school-based mentoring.

- The main value university-based teacher education can bring to the development of professional judgement is in bringing professional judgement into relief and making its associated skills and dispositions more visible as core elements of teaching. In addition, it can emphasise the importance of facilitating reflection on relationships between propositional and procedural ways of knowing. Experience alone is no guarantee of professional development. Experiences must be filtered through reflection to capitalise on their value. Teacher educators certainly could do more to support professional development in this area.

- It is important for novice teachers to become able to reason about both specific critical classroom incidents and more global classroom trends. On top of this, the ability to understand how the former influences the latter, and vice versa, is critical to the development of teacher expertise. The key to this is adapting both micro- and macro-level mindsets and micro- and macro-level visions for one's practice.

- Key roles for teacher educators and early career mentors include shaping mindsets, facilitating opportunities and encouraging reflection.

CHAPTER 5 | JUDGEMENTS ABOUT WHAT? ANALYSIS OF SOME CASE STUDIES

CRITICAL ISSUES

- *What do real-life judgements look and feel like to novice teachers?*
- *How might teacher educators and school mentors make use of the assertions and advice about the necessity of professional judgements and ways it can be nurtured that are presented in Chapters 2 and 4?*
- *What habits of mind are useful for novices, pre-service teachers and their mentors to develop?*
- *What obstacles might prevent teacher educators and school mentors from becoming more effective in nurturing professional judgement?*

Introduction

Chapter 4 finished with some recommendations for ways teacher educators and school mentors could draw on the frameworks of judgements 1 and 2 to support their decision-making *on* and *in* moments of teaching. In this chapter, I present a series of real-life case studies describing actual events, drawn from interviews with trainees and practitioners in a variety of education contexts. Each case study is analysed to identify the judgements made (or not made) and ways teacher educators and school mentors could capitalise on them to support the novice teacher, drawing on suggestions from Chapter 4. There are also questions for teacher educators and school mentors which prompt them to reflect on the case studies and consider how they might achieve this. Following the case studies, I discuss some factors, practical and political, which prevent teacher educators and school mentors from nurturing professional judgement as freely as they might like.

CASE STUDY 1

Jennifer

Jennifer is an early career teacher (ECT) teaching physical education (PE) in a large suburban secondary school. In a Year 8 (12- to 13-year-olds) hockey lesson on the school field Jennifer is teaching passing and ball control skills to 26 pupils. After a brief group warm up, Jennifer uses a pupil to help her demonstrate the first drill, executing a push-pass to your partner who controls the ball and push-passes it back. Jennifer talks through the techniques involved, asks for any questions and then instructs the pupils to pair up, spread out into space on the field and begin rehearsing the drill. Some pupils pair up quickly, while others discus and argue about pairing up for a few minutes. Eventually, Jennifer intervenes and directs some of the pairings, including making a group of three. Within a few more minutes, most of the pupils are passing the ball between them, with varying degrees of success. However, Jennifer notices several pairs who are not attempting the technique she demonstrated at all but appear to be swinging wildly at the ball and returning it without controlling it first. Others have invented their own passing games and a few pairs have joined to form a group game. To encourage them to attempt the technique, she blows her whistle, stops everyone and shouts (because now the pupils are spread out across the whole field) an instruction for all pairs to follow the technique from her demonstration. She asks if everyone remembers it and some pupils shake their heads. Using a pair near her who were doing it correctly, she instructs the whole group to watch them demonstrate the technique. Blowing her whistle again, she sets the pupils off to continue rehearsing the passing and control, though the success rate does not improve a great deal over the following ten minutes. Concerned about time and knowing that she has more drills to cover in this lesson, Jennifer calls the pupils in to her and moves onto the next part of the lesson.

Reflecting on this lesson later with her mentor, Jennifer was quite downcast and negative, feeling that the lesson objectives had not been met and that she had not managed the activities very well. Her mentor responded by pointing out that teaching is essentially a series of judgement calls in response to dilemmas which present themselves. In helping Jennifer to see her mistakes as starting points for future success, her mentor's starting point was to encourage her to go back through the lesson in her head and pinpoint the specific dilemmas she faced. Next, they spent some time discussing each dilemma, the possible options it presented and the usefulness of Jennifer's judgements. Her mentor was able to point out some of the very useful judgements Jennifer made, including checking for understanding by questioning before spreading the pupils out and using pupils to help demonstrate skills, as well as some of the less effective ones, such as shouting instructions across the field. Finally, Jennifer's mentor encouraged her to consider which of these judgements could have been made prior to the lesson, at the planning stage (judgement 1) and which could only be made during the lesson (judgement 2).

Reflection point

»   Identify the dilemmas which presented themselves to Jennifer. Read through the case study again and try to list all the moments where Jennifer was faced with multiple options for how to proceed.

With some prompts from her mentor, Jennifer came up with the following list. Does your list look anything like Jennifer's?

» How to demonstrate the drill?

» Let the pupils choose pairs or put them in pairs?

» When to spread the pupils out?

    o Do they know/understand enough?

» How to communicate to the pupils once they're spread out in the environment?

    o Stop them and bring them into me?

    o Shout instructions?

» How to address misunderstandings across a wide-open environment?

» Judging who is/is not being successful?

» Determining why pupils are not successful?

    o Lack of skill/co-ordination?

    o Lack of listening?

    o Subverting the lesson?

» When to cut losses and move onto the next drill?

» How to reinforce behavioural expectations without creating a negative atmosphere?

» How much time to spend on each part of the lesson?

» How to give independence to the pupils without wasting valuable teaching and learning time?

Reflection point

Notice that Jennifer's mentor did not tell her what she should have done. Furlong (2015) points out that professional expectations and standards for teachers are usually articulated in terms of what teachers should do but neglect the development of the far more important professional skills of judgement and reasoning. It is to the mentor's credit in this case study that he elicited post hoc judgements about key dilemmas in the lesson from Jennifer, rather than simply telling her. This is more time-consuming, but far more developmentally useful.

A particular contextual challenge central to Jennifer's case study is the expanded teaching environment. Managing the complex range of variables involved in a lesson for 25 pupils is made considerably harder when they are necessarily spread out into a wide available space. The openness of the outdoor environment amplified the complexity and presented additional practical challenges, with which Jennifer struggled. However, the teaching environment was among the factors which were known in advance of the lesson and therefore some of these challenges could have been mitigated with some category 1 judgements during the lesson-planning stage. A useful habit of mind for Jennifer and other novice teachers to develop in such instances is to think ahead and begin to pre-reason about features of the lesson which may create difficulties. One of the most powerful approaches which Jennifer's mentor took was to encourage her to separate judgement 1 and 2 dilemmas in her reflections. This exercise carries potentially significant professional learning for the novice teacher, as they are challenged to consider which dilemmas could have been anticipated in advance, and which not.

Reflection point

> » Looking at Jennifer's list of dilemmas, identify which may have been foreseeable at the planning stage (requiring judgement 1) and which were more likely to emerge during the lesson (requiring judgement 2).

Storey and Butler (2010) made the observation that teaching and learning games in PE lessons inevitably involve elements of self-organisation. In wide open spaces, pupils feel a greater sense of autonomy, which in turn tends to bring about individual and collective invention. Pupils are more likely to become creative and adaptive (or subversive) in this context than, for example, when seated in a classroom, partly due to their proximity to the teacher, but also the greater available physical space in which to operate. Managing or capitalising on such 'open systems', as Doll (1993) calls them, can be demanding for novice teachers and an extremely useful concept for those nurturing their professional judgement to draw on is 'enabling constraints' (Biesta, 2009). Enabling constraints are organisational parameters built into teaching and learning which facilitate active pupil engagement while militating against excessive complexity. Davis and Sumara (2006, p 145) describe them in the following way:

the structural conditions that help to determine the balance between sources of coherence that allow a collective to maintain a focus of purpose/identity and sources of disruption and randomness that compel the collective to constantly adjust and adapt.

Enabling constraints may include pupil groupings, tasks, resources, pace and timing, physical environment or, as discussed in Chapter 3, organisational structures (centralised, decentralised, distributed). In the context of a PE lesson on a sports field, knowing how and when to manipulate enabling constraints and developing an instinct for managing interrelationships between coherence and randomness are crucial. Reviewing the advice for school mentors from Chapter 4, it seems that Jennifer's mentor encouraged her to think about this by applying the following recommendations.

> » Allocate time for reflection on judgements novices made during their teaching.

> » Support novices to distinguish between judgements which can be made while planning and judgements which can only be made in the moment.

» Resist the temptation (and it is a significant temptation) to simply *tell* novices what to do (or what they ought to have done). Instead, it is more powerful and productive for mentors to:

   o   talk and reason about their own thought processes;

   o   elicit reasoning from novices;

   o   where they do give specific advice, always offer explanations.

CASE **STUDY 2**

Zayd

Zayd is in his fifth year of teaching and his first year working in a Special Educational Needs and Disabilities (SEND) school. The school caters for pupils aged 5–16 who have a variety of complex additional needs. Zayd teaches class 11 (10- to 12-year-olds) and is supported by a teaching assistant (TA). While Zayd is not a novice teacher, this is his first experience of teaching in the special needs' sector, and as such, he has been allocated a more senior colleague as a mentor for this academic year.

During one of Zayd's lessons, a pupil from his class, who had been outside in the corridor having refused to participate in a lesson, became angry and smashed the glass window of the classroom door. He then entered the class-room shouting and holding a piece of broken glass and was clearly in a dis-tressed and unpredictable state. Concerned about the safety of all the pupils, Zayd asked his TA to remove the other ten pupils from the classroom and close the door behind them. With just himself and the distressed pupil in the room and recognising that the pupil's psychological goals were to gain atten-tion and control, Zayd began pretending to work on his computer at his desk, in his words to '*create the impression of composure and "normality"*'. Meanwhile the pupil began tipping over tables, climbing on tables and hitting the ceiling tiles with a metre ruler. Apparently frustrated by the lack of attention coming from Zayd, he then pulled the computer plug from its socket. With the com-puter now off, Zayd began writing on his notepad and checking emails on his phone. Eventually, having not received either attention or control for his negative behaviour, the pupil became calm and started talking to Zayd, asking questions like '*When is it lunch time?*' and '*What are we doing next week?*' almost as if nothing had happened. After some time, Zayd was able to bring the conversation around to the repair work which was needed in the classroom and, considering the extremity of the behaviour, was satisfied when the pupil had put a few tables and chairs back the correct way and in their correct posi-tions. Zayd remained with the pupil until lunch time at which point he took him to the headteacher's office.

Reflection point

» Make a list of the judgements Zayd was required to make during this incident.

» If you were the senior colleague mentoring Zayd in school, what would your priorities be during a post-incident professional dialogue?

Unpredictable events such as this are principally the territory of judgement 2. When such incidents arise, a teacher's prior experiences and the knowledge they engender about individual pupils are invaluable and necessary sources of judgement. However, in the heat of the moment, effective in situ judgement (judgement 2) is a teacher's leading tool. In this instance, Zayd encountered and navigated a series of quite high-stake challenges and judgement calls, including (in no particular order):

» judgements about severity of the situation (assessing risk);

» managing his own emotions;

» managing pupils' and support staff's emotions;

» managing the short game (what's immediately in front of him) and the long game (the consequences of what is happening);

» deciding who will do what;

» managing safety, including his own;

» reasoning about what 'repair work' would be needed and how to achieve it (Zayd used the term 'repair work' a number of times during the interview referring to something like restorative justice);

» constant prioritising – judging which actions are most important moment by moment;

» how much/whether to engage with the pupil once in a one-to-one situation.

Let's analyse a couple of these and try to derive some useful insights about the support a school mentor could offer in similar circumstances.

Managing the short game and the long game

Reasoning about immediate and longer-term events and consequences is another vital habit of mind which permeates all aspects of teaching. As such, it is one of the things about which teachers spend a considerable amount of time making judgements. Such judgements typically revolve around two questions.

1. What actions must I take immediately in response to events unfolding right now? *(What can/should I solve immediately?)*

2. What actions will need to follow subsequently to resolve or progress the situation positively? *(What can't be solved immediately, but must be addressed later?)*

These questions apply to behaviour management, as in Zayd's case study, but also to aspects of pupil learning like misconceptions, incorrect answers, procedural misunderstandings or peer-to-peer cooperation, planning and assessment. Rehearsing and reflecting upon distinguishing between immediate and follow-up actions presents some powerful professional learning opportunities which can unlock teacher expertise.

Reflection point

A possible mentor follow-up is to ask the novice teacher to reflect back on a critical incident and disentangle the necessary immediate, from the follow-up actions. Mentors could talk about the value of being able to play both the short and long games.

Engaging with the pupil in a one-to-one situation

Once the rest of the class had vacated the classroom, Zayd was left alone with the pupil in question. The goal of restoring calm and beginning to engage the pupil constructively presented some interesting dilemmas. Zayd's in situ judgements drew on theory about underlying psychological goals, previous experience of the pupil and some improvisation in the form of what I refer to as a sort of dead reckoning. Dead reckoning was a navigational practice used by mariners before it was possible to precisely calculate a vessel's position at sea. During dead reckoning, the current position of a moving object (like a ship) was determined by using a previously known position as a point of reference and making estimates of speed, direction and time. Rough calculations were made in response to knowledge about prior calculations. In a similar way, Zayd determined the most productive course of action by trying something (pretending to answer emails), then judging from the pupils' response whether to maintain or change course. Trialling teacher actions, getting feedback from the environment, evaluating the feedback and determining how to proceed are common means of judging how best to proceed in a variety of classroom situations. Reading Zayd's experience in this case study is similar to Shulman's (2004, p 436) description of teaching as '*an exquisitely complex form of reasoning and judgement*'; the teacher reasons about the consequences of their actions and judges the next steps accordingly, and it certainly is complex. This is one of the reasons trainee and novice teachers find placements and early career stages so tiring; reflective teachers are always assessing the usefulness of actions and events and judging what to say or do next; always thinking a few steps ahead.

CASE **STUDY 3**

Lucy

Lucy is a postgraduate teacher education student on her final assessed placement in a Year 4 class in England. Lucy's case study is an excerpt of responses she gave during a research focus group interview. She was one of four teacher education students responding to questions for a study looking at trainee teachers' experiences of autonomy and judgement while on final teaching practice placements. Her responses paint a picture which many student teachers, their lecturers and school mentors may recognise.

Researcher: *How comfortable do you feel taking risks or trying things out in your lessons? And what enables or prevents you from doing so?*

Lucy: *I really quite enjoy taking risks and trying new things, but in the context of, for example, maths or English, I'm quite nervous to take risks because my teacher is really good and so her expectations, not of me, necessarily, but of children, are quite high. The school expects me to be quite faithful to the curriculum scheme they use. In terms of the curriculum, I would have quite enjoyed going off piste a little bit but didn't really feel like they wanted me to do that. I chose not to take risks very often because I wanted to do a good job and be evaluated highly.*

Researcher: *Right. And what are the specific factors which influenced that choice?*

Lucy: *Relationship with my class mentor and wanting that to be positive. Not wanting it to seem that I don't like her ideas and I want to try my own ideas and then if it goes terribly, she may say, 'Well, I told you so!' But also, just wanting to pass and not have to redo lessons. Not having a bad comment on my report maybe. I think generally I'm a risk taker in life, but when it comes to feeling I have little autonomy; it just limits how much I'm willing to try things, knowing that actually the school and the university are kind of trusting me to do a good job. It makes me less keen to take risks in a way that once I'm a teacher I'll be much happier to do; when there's nobody watching me.*

There is plenty to unpack from this short episode which is illustrative of a common phenomenon experienced by class mentors and student teachers alike during teaching placements. Lucy appears to have put limits on her own professional judgements because of her position as a visitor in her placement classroom. Factors such as not wanting to irritate her class mentor, concerns about how making her own judgements might negatively affect her gradings and the high-stake reality of being observed and scrutinised have discouraged her from using her own initiative. Many years of mentoring student teachers on placements, observing them teach and engaging in feedback discussions have taught me that almost all feel like Lucy to some degree. In many ways, this is simply a fact of life when on teaching practice, and it would be rare to find a student teacher who enjoys similar levels of autonomy and scope for exercising professional judgement as a qualified or experienced teacher. However, that is not to say it is not problematic for novices learning how to develop teacher expertise. At its most extreme, a lack of permission to trial one's ideas and experience the success or failure which follows can stifle a novice teacher's professional development. Burn et al (2015) point out that professional relationships between trainees and their mentors are complex because of the roles each inhabit and the expectations these roles engender. For example, it is easy for support and advice from a mentor to be misconstrued by a trainee because of the role the mentor also plays as assessor. In Lucy's case, the stifling appeared to be more self-imposed than imposed by her mentor; however, finding a balance between the necessity for trainees to follow an experienced professional's lead and the necessity for rehearsal of judgements is crucial for the developing teacher. As suggested in Chapter 2, trainees' and novice teachers' sense of permission to judge and decide is key in unlocking both categories of judgement. Hara and Sherbine (2018) are among several others who have noted the developmental challenges trainees face when they are not afforded sufficient latitude to explore pedagogical ideas. However, locating that sweet spot between what we might call 'top-down parameters' and 'bottom-up invention' is difficult for both mentors and trainees. The drivers for a mentor who is reluctant to hand over the reins are well known:

» the right of all pupils to be taught to a high standard;

» the pressure of pupil attainment targets and exams;

» a desire to maintain a calm, productive and co-operative classroom environment;

» a fear of giving up control of these factors;

» the mentor's own professional appraisal;

» the buck stopping with the mentor.

These are legitimate concerns for class teachers mentoring student teachers, and I can remember the effects these factors had on me when I was a teacher with trainees on placement in my class. However, managing these top-down and bottom-up factors does not have to be a zero-sum game; there are ways of achieving a helpful balance between the two, such as the following.

» High-quality initial mentoring of class mentors can go a long way to establish the expectation that the process of developing as a teacher necessitates opportunities for autonomy and professional decision making.

» Trainee preparation for placements should include teaching about the developmental value of exercising autonomous judgement, and expectation management about realistic levels of autonomy with reference to their stage of training.

» Negotiation about levels of autonomy must form part of regular professional dialogue between trainees and their mentors, so that trainees understand mentors' reasoning for the levels of autonomy they give, and mentors understand trainees' confidence, desire and willingness to exercise autonomy.

In essence, autonomy for trainees on placement should not be an elephant in the room, but a topic for open discussion and constant review. Considering this, a productive habit of mind for trainees is to be seeking opportunities to exercise their judgement within a realistic developmental framework, and for mentors a useful mindset is to begin with the intention of offering every realistic judgement opportunity to those they mentor, expanding or contracting opportunities as appropriate. Another way of thinking about this from a mentor's perspective is to say that within what is realistic from a school point of view, a successful mentor will allow for as much autonomy as the trainee or novice can make productive developmental use of, without experiencing detrimental failures or compromising pupils' education in the medium to long term. This is an important element of building decisional capital (see Chapter 2) in developing teachers.

CASE STUDY 4

Angela

Angela is in the first year of an initial teacher education degree and on placement in an early years setting. One morning a few weeks into the placement, having familiarised herself with the classroom routines and having developed good relationships with the pupils, she is interacting with a four-year-old boy called Edward. Her mentor is observing the interaction and will give Angela feedback afterwards. Edward is using a digger toy in the sandpit to dig, move and tip sand in different locations. Angela is crouched by the sandpit with him. As he plays, he verbalises a commentary on what he is doing and why and the following exchange occurs.

Edward: [digging with the digger bucket to pick up sand] *I have to dig deep to get all the rubble in my bucket.*

Angela: *Oh yes, that's good.*

Edward: *This bucket is big so it can dig deep.*

Angela: *Yes. Are you going to build a house?*

Edward: *Where's the dumper truck? Oh, there. That's why I have to dump this load in the dump truck.* [Puts the truck on the other side of the sandpit.]

Angela: *Do you like working on the building site?*

Edward: *It's not a building site, it's a quarry.* [Makes engine noises as he drives the digger to the dump truck.]

Angela: *Oh, I thought you were building a house.*

Edward: *You're the dumper truck driver. You have to go backwards while I tip the rubble in there.*

Angela: *OK, then I'll dump it on this pile.* [Starts to tip the sand out.]

Edward: *No. It's not full up yet. I need to put more rubble in first.*

Angela: *Oh, right. OK.*

While reflecting on this short episode later with her mentor, Angela admitted that she didn't feel confident about her role or what was expected of her. She had already witnessed several similar one-to-one interactions between pupils and her mentor but felt unsure if what she was doing was appropriate. Her mentor reassured her that this had been a fun and useful episode of play for Edward and that Angela did not do anything wrong. However, there were some ways to develop her interactive skills for future episodes.

Reflection point

» If you were Angela's mentor, how would you guide her to a better understanding of her role in one-to-one play-based interactions, without simply telling her what to do?

Due to the generally less prescriptive curricula and the underlying principle of following children's interests, teaching in the early years tends to involve even more in situ judgements (judgement 2) than teaching in the later years. Any experienced early years teacher will attest to making moment-by-moment judgements and adjustments constantly throughout a typical day. It can be quite exhausting. Unlike Lucy in the previous case study, Angela's mentor had created conditions in which she felt permitted to exercise her judgement (see Chapter 4). Her challenge was feeling unsure about her overall aims. In this case study, Angela had a range of in situ judgements to make, mostly concerning how she responded to Edward's utterances; however, without a clear sense of what she was hoping to achieve, she found it difficult to judge how best to respond. This is illustrative of an important feature of any judgement. While judgements can be instinctive and more intuitive than explicit, and though there is always an improvisatory element to professional judgements, they are not whims. Judgements are rooted in knowledge and experience and are a means to a known and understood (even if tacitly) end. This point is emphasised in Chapter 2 when introducing the model for factors contributing to category 2 judgements. Experience, disciplinary knowledge, structures and rubrics play important roles in the development of in situ judgement. In Angela's case, as a first-year trainee, she lacked the experience, knowledge about early learning and development and knowledge of early years teaching frameworks to understand the ends she was aiming for and therefore fully capitalise on her interaction with Edward. A useful starting point for her mentor would have been to look at the Early Learning Goals in the Early Years Foundation Stage (EYFS) (DfE, 2021a) framework. Knowledge of the rubric for Communication and Language, for example, would have enabled Angela to judge and formulate her responses to Edward with the aims of supporting him to do the following.

» *Offer explanations for why things might happen.*

» *Make use of recently introduced vocabulary.*

» *Express [his] ideas and feelings about [his] experiences using full sentences, including use of past, present and future tenses and making use of conjunctions.*

(DfE, 2021a, p 11)

Had the episode been videoed (as recommended in Chapter 4) another powerful learning experience would have been to ask Angela to rewatch it and note the points where she could have responded differently to elicit more language rehearsal and development from Edward. At the end of Chapter 4, I suggested that teacher educators must encourage trainees to engage in post-placement reflections about the skills and dispositions which unlock expert judgements. Top of this list was reflections on the value of internalised knowledge of the intended destination and planned routes for a lesson.

Angela's case study shows the importance of this professional disposition. It also serves as a useful reminder that the development of such dispositions is mediated by reflection, as illustrated by the models for judgements 1 and 2 shown in Figure 5.1. Post hoc reflection with a mentor while on placement and post-placement reflection with teacher educators are crucial to the development of the knowledge, skills and dispositions required to develop expert judgement. Schön's (1983) theory of reflection *in* and *on* moments of action emphasises that the two types of reflection (or perhaps times of reflection) are qualitatively different and serve different purposes. While reflections *in* action invite individuals to judge the best responses in the moment using information available in the moment (judgement 2), reflections *on* action invite individuals to make judgements about future action based on knowledge accumulated from previous actions, system constraints (such as curriculum) and theory. In Angela's case, a thorough understanding of the age-related curriculum learning and development goals would help her to plan effectively for future sustained shared dialogue with young children. The combination of reflections on past interactions, curriculum goals and significant pedagogical principles (ie following the child's lead) would begin to unlock the habits of expertise in judgements 1 and 2.

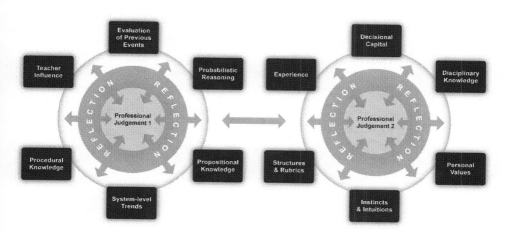

Figure 5.1 The mediating role of reflection in category 1 and category 2 professional judgements

Obstacles to the nurturing of novice teacher judgement

As mentioned in Chapter 2, lacking a sense of permission commonly discourages some novice (and some experienced) teachers from exercising their professional judgement. Sometimes this lack of permission is articulated explicitly, but often this message is indirectly *felt* more than directly or explicitly received by teachers. Descriptors of what quality teaching looks like in England, such as the TS (DfE, 2021b) or the Early Career Framework (ECF) (DfE, 2019a), give no explicit instructions for teachers not to make judgements about their work. The problem, and the reason many novice teachers lack a sense of approval, is that these policies actually make no explicit mention of judgement at all. The absence of any mention of teacher judgement in the policies which describe best practice is problematic for novices and their mentors for several reasons.

First, it creates the impression to novices that best practice teacher actions just appear out of nowhere, as if they are things teachers simply do, or don't do. As noted in Chapter 2, any given teacher action has a range of judgements behind it; however, without unambiguous reference to judgement in professional descriptors, the novice can be left in the dark about how to achieve the standards against which they are to be assessed. For school mentors and teacher educators, the problem is that teacher education curricula (the Core Content Framework (CCF) (DfE, 2019b) and the early career mentoring frameworks (ECF) (DfE, 2019a)) draw significantly on professional standards policy and what is absent from the policy is likely to be absent from the curricula. The consequence of this is that the dilemmas, decisions, reasoning and judgement underlying expert teaching are rarely, if ever, mentioned during teacher education or the first few probationary years of qualified teaching. Take these examples from the TS and ECF.

Teachers' Standard 5. Adapt teaching to respond to the strengths and needs of all pupils

- *Know when and how to differentiate appropriately, using approaches which enable pupils to be taught effectively.*

(DfE, 2021b, p 11)

ECF Section 4 Classroom Practice – Learn how to plan effective lessons, by

- *Removing scaffolding only when pupils are achieving a high degree of success in applying previously taught material.*

(DfE, 2019a, p 15)

In the first example from the TS, the phrase '*know when and how to*' is quite misleading as it implies that differentiation (or adaptive practice to use the current terminology) is fixed knowledge to be acquired by trainees. Since appropriate ways and moments to adapt teaching to meet pupils' needs are likely to be highly contextual and even unique to particular instances, '*knowing how and when*' could helpfully be replaced by '*judging how and when*'. This shifts the emphasis away from adopting inert knowledge towards something more like evaluating and deciding how to act, which is developmentally far more useful for trainees and novices. The second example from the ECF describes something which teachers at all age phases do daily, gradually adapting or removing learner scaffolds. As with the example from the TS though, it is presented like a piece of discrete knowledge one should simply know how to apply. However, knowing how and when to do this is a matter of practical judgement. Unlike other professional disciplines such as medicine or social work, in teaching (in England at least) the professional's judgement is conspicuously missing from the documents which inform their professional development.

This creates another barrier to the development of professional judgement, opportunities to rehearse. If professional judgement is not formally emphasised in policy and therefore not regularly promoted and supported in teacher education, opportunities to rehearse it, reflect on it and develop it may be scant. Of course, to some extent, a trainee or novice's judgement is always being rehearsed while operating in the classroom. However, to be developed fully, rehearsal needs to take the form of what Ericsson and Moxley (2012) refer to as deliberate practice which is explicit, effortful and reflected upon.

Perhaps the most significant obstacle to the conditions and practices which might encourage the development of professional judgement is time. Teacher educators, and especially teachers themselves, are usually extraordinarily busy as are trainee and novice teachers, which means that the sort of developmental opportunities and experiences I have advocated in this book can (and sometimes do) fall by the wayside. Watching, unpicking and reflecting on videoed practice for example is not rare because it is not useful, but because finding time to do it can be extremely difficult. In this case, I would disagree with the well-known observation that to achieve great things, two things are needed: a plan and not quite enough time (Anon). Those training and mentoring teachers certainly need a plan for nurturing judgement, but they also need enough time. For school mentors, this demands excellent and creative time management, a firm belief in the value of judgement in teaching and a determination to nurture it. In teacher education it means navigating the various compliance agendas which comprise much of the curriculum, including systematic synthetic phonics training, curriculum subject coverage, subject content knowledge, behaviour management, Special Educational Needs and Disabilities (SEND) and English as an additional language (EAL) as well as training in safeguarding, prevention of radicalisation (Prevent) and promoting fundamental British values. Of course, judgement is relevant to all of these areas, which suggests a useful strategy would be to build it into the fabric of a teacher education programme as an underlying pedagogical principle. In theory, if teacher judgement enjoyed a more prominent position in descriptors of expert teaching, each of these obstacles, including the conundrum of time, would seem less daunting.

Encouragingly, however, though the language of judgement is conspicuously scant in teacher education and early career policy, the language of reflection is common. Thanks in no small part to the seminal work of Donald Schön, and more recently in teacher education, Andrew Pollard, reflection is firmly embedded in the fabric of teacher education and development. As an example of this, compared to '*judgement*' which isn't mentioned once in the CCF, '*reflect*' appears five times. '*Judgement*' also makes no appearance in the ECF, though '*reflect*' appears twice. In the TS '*judgement*' appears twice, but only in reference to headteachers judging trainee's teaching, whereas '*reflection*' is mentioned four times. These numbers are not large, but they illustrate how reflection has become a part of the furniture (so to speak) in policy and therefore an expected skill for trainee and novice teachers to develop. In contrast, in the Australian Professional Standards for Teaching (AITSL, 2018) the term '*judgement*' appears frequently in the context of assessment and professional conduct.

Focus area 5.2 Provide feedback to students on their learning

- *Select from an effective range of strategies to provide targeted feedback based on informed and timely judgements of each student's current needs in order to progress learning.*

Standard 7: Engage professionally with colleagues, parents/carers and the community

- *Model exemplary ethical behaviour and exercise informed judgements in all professional dealings with students, colleagues and the community.*

(AITSL, 2018, pp 18 and 22)

There are many areas of the Australian rubric where judgement is conspicuously absent; however, it is encouraging to see its inclusion in a best-practice publication, albeit minimal. Emphasising the complex and contingent nature of teaching and learning in this way can be daunting because it rightly implies that there are few fixed correct actions or responses (though there may be known incorrect ones, especially in the case of professional conduct). However, it can also be empowering for teachers at all career stages because it foregrounds the necessity of their judgement, their agency. In my view, a worthwhile policy and curricular development in teacher education would be for the concept (and practice) of exercising judgement to accompany reflection, as two sides of the same coin. The purpose of reflection is to inform action, and between reflections and actions lie *judgements*.

IN A **NUTSHELL**

This chapter has contextualised some of the complexities of teaching described in Chapters 2 and 3 and has shown how proposed advice for teacher educators and school mentors from Chapter 4 might be applied in practice. In different ways, the four case studies illustrate the crucial role that reflection plays in making judgements about actions, both in the future (judgement 1) and in the moment (judgement 2). They also show how teaching is essentially an ongoing process of facing and managing multiple professional dilemmas. Finally, they demonstrate the central role that effective teaching and mentoring play in nurturing judgement.

REFLECTIONS ON **CRITICAL ISSUES**

- Real-life professional judgements can look daunting and feel uncomfortable to trainee and novice teachers. This is partly because learning to make useful and productive judgements takes time, involves making mistakes and demands effortful reflection. However, it is also because in the training and development of novice teachers we have yet to afford judgement the status or attention it warrants. This leaves many novices feeling unsure and unconfident.

- Teacher educators and school mentors would benefit enormously in their training and support for novice teachers by having professional descriptors and best-practice rubrics which make more prominent reference to professional judgement with clarity about its central role in the development of expert teaching. Time is a significant obstacle to some of the reflective practices which encourage skills in judgement. However, professional dialogue which frames expert teaching as dilemma management is a useful habit of mind for novices and their mentors because it emphasises the contingent nature of classroom pedagogy and the value of judgement.

CHAPTER 6 | CONCLUSION

The hallmark of a profession is the presence of enormously complex and indeterminate problem situations, and the exercise of professional judgement characterises such practice.

Shulman (2004, p 253)

Introduction

This book has presented arguments for the value and necessity of teachers exercising professional judgement in their classroom practice. In essence, these arguments can be encapsulated by the following two propositions.

1. Learning is a complex, non-linear and contingent phenomenon, which is influenced by a networked array of factors, from within and outside of schools and classrooms. Learning is not entirely predictable and does not always appear on cue.

2. Effective teaching, therefore, cannot follow a predetermined script. It is a judgement-dependent activity, the aim of which is to problematise that indeterminacy in the interests of learning.

The book has also advanced assertions about the necessary conditions for pre-service and novice teachers to learn to exercise their judgement. These can best be summarised by the concepts of permission and capability. The permission condition involves more than simply the knowledge (explicitly given or simply felt) that one has sufficient decisional capital to make discretionary judgements, though this is vital. It also includes an understanding that judgement is expected; that it is a professional obligation. Throughout the book, I have tried to demonstrate that both these aspects of permission can only be realised fully when messages about the central role which judgement plays in teaching permeate the profession at all stages and levels. This includes teacher education curricula, teacher professional standards, school inspection frameworks, school leadership and classroom practice mentoring. Following on from this, the capability condition demands that those teaching and mentoring trainee and novice teachers emphasise the role which judgement plays and are themselves able to make useful judgements about how much discretionary autonomy rookie teachers can make productive use of. In short, capability in exercising judgements develops through being taught and having some licence to judge in the classroom. Fledgling professionals need, to paraphrase Doll (1989), a profitable balance of dancing and marching. Currently, with their reliance on somewhat inert depictions of teaching as doing and learning as product, with minimal acknowledgement of the necessity of judgement, trainees and novices in England, and some comparable education systems, are doing more marching than dancing.

In its own way, each chapter of the book has illustrated just how demanding it is to teach a class of children and made suggestions about ways in which professional judgement lies at the heart of effective teaching. These range from acknowledging classroom complexity to foregrounding judgement as vital to teachers' pedagogical toolkit, prioritising reflection, allowing novices to make mistakes and adapting policy. There is still much to be improved on with these systems supporting pre-service and novice teachers. Though there are many excellent teachers who exercise their judgement expertly moment by moment while they work, I would argue that they do so more despite, than because of, these systems. The skills of professional judgement should not be something teachers stumble across incidentally or develop arbitrarily, if at all. To be capitalised upon fully in the interest of pupils' learning, teachers should be aware of their significance, conscious of what is developing and how, and deliberate in their pursuit of it. The following sections draw on points made throughout the book to present portraits of what university-based initial teacher education (ITE) and school-based early career mentoring might look like if professional judgement was deliberately emphasised.

Judgement in ITE: a future aspiration

I have argued in Chapter 5 that for judgement to become an embedded, everyday element of ITE it would need to enjoy a more prominent position in the policies which guide teacher preparation. This means the TS (DfE, 2021b), the CCF (DfE, 2019b) and the ECF (2019a) would employ the language of complexity, subtlety, unpredictability and judgement. This would subtly reframe how teacher educators and their students think about teaching, how they talk about and reflect on practice and how professional development trajectories are conceptualised. For trainees who are supported to understand teaching as navigating a wide range of dilemmas, requiring a series of judgements both *in* and *on* the moment, reflections on their development would shift towards evaluating strengths and weaknesses in their interpretation and response to the processes of pupil learning. In this future aspiration, professional development itself is also framed more convincingly as a learning journey and less as a race to an idealised finish line which one either has crossed or is yet to cross. This does not mean that descriptions of ideal practice or outcomes are not valuable; they undoubtedly are. However, descriptions of the finish line should share policy space with descriptions of the journey.

Trainees reflecting on their judgements would be encouraged to discuss the decisions they make while planning lessons or while teaching, exploring and articulating the reasoning behind them. When preparing written, oral, portfolio or any form of assessment, trainees would analyse and discuss, but also take for granted, the complex nature of learning and its complex and nuanced relationship to teaching. Phrases like '*teachers should*' would feature rarely, unless accompanied by words like '*interpret*', '*judge*', '*problematise*', '*experiment*', '*decide*', '*select*', '*evaluate*' or '*reflect*' to name just a few possibilities. Implications for professional development would be discussed in terms of progression in sound judgement, acknowledging that this might mean different things in different classroom contexts.

Linking theory and practice would be central and ubiquitous throughout such a teacher education programme because professional judgement is like the glue which binds theoretical and practical knowledge. As my model for type 1 professional judgement shows, propositional (knowing *that*) and procedural (knowing *how*) knowledge are necessary ingredients for successful classroom judgements. Not only that, but they must also be mutually influential. Trainees would be encouraged and supported to build their knowledge of learning and teaching theories, including criticisms of them, to sharpen their propositional understanding against which their procedural experiences and judgements can be interrogated, and vice versa. The common mantra that theory and practice in teacher education appear fragmented (Yin, 2019; Karlsson Lohmander, 2015), even mutually exclusive, would rarely be expressed. A focus on decisional judgement, while in or removed from the moment of teaching, necessitates the unpicking of practice using theory and the critical analysis of theory using practice. As Helleve et al (2021, p 2) point out, the '*gap*' between theory and practice exists because '*every situation in practice is unique and there is no recipe for how a teacher should react*'. Judgement provides a basis for school-based experiences to be mediated in university programmes and vice versa. As Campbell and Dunleavy (2016) have argued, it is not more time in school, or in university, which would most benefit pre-service teachers, but meaningful integration of the two. Problematising judgement bridges this so-called '*gap*'.

Since in this future aspiration, articulations of expertise in professional standards policies emphasise the importance of judgement, trainee teachers are assessed not only on the outcomes of their teaching, but also on the judgements they make and their reflections on them. A key question when assessing trainees' teaching progress is not only '*how well are pupils learning?*' but also (and just as importantly) '*is the aspiring teacher becoming one who can judge what is best?*' The next section describes what mentoring looks like for these trainees when they enter the profession.

Judgement in early career mentoring: a future aspiration

Trainees educated with this emphasis on professional judgement become novices who appreciate the range of sources on which they can draw to support their decisions about planning for and facilitating pupils' learning. They and their mentors understand that skills associated with judgement take time to unfold and that missteps and poor judgements can be fertile ground for reflection and future successes. Such mentoring of early career teachers naturally involves evaluation of the quality and impact of their teaching, but it also takes account of the complex and unpredictable nature of the classroom, and of pupils' learning. This means acknowledging that there is no silver bullet or single right approach to any given teaching and learning situation. It means reinforcing the idea that a range of reasonable choices can be made and that choosing the most appropriate will be a question of judgement guided by multiple domains of knowledge. This is what Coles (2002) refers to as doing what is *best* rather than what is *right*.

Guided by policy frameworks which do not present learning as simply a linear product of teaching (Strom and Mitchell Viesca, 2020) and which employ the language of professional judgement, mentors would support novices towards conscious competence in exercising their adaptive expertise. This means drawing attention to the many daily decisional cross-roads at which novices arrive, reflecting on their judgements, and consequences of their judgements, so that they become attentive to the habits (useful or otherwise) they are developing. This requires a focus on process as well as on product. Expert mentors would also share their own professional judgements and, while resisting the urge to tell novices what to do, impart aspects of their own pedagogical acumen by explaining the thinking behind decisions made in their classrooms. Without allowing the novice to make errors which may be terminal to their confidence or compromise pupils' education, the model this mentorship most closely resembles is that of coaching. When judgement is empha-sised as the principal vehicle for the development of professional expertise, conditions are created in which novice teachers can, in the words of Wallace et al (2021, p 407), be empowered to 'experiment, risk-take and engage directly with learner outcomes'. Skilful judgement-focused mentors (rather than solely competency-focused mentors) would help novices to understand their practice, what motivates it, what assumptions it is built upon, why it works, why it fails, how they can make changes and how to evaluate them. This is in contrast to mentoring which only highlights the quality of practice in relation to predefined competencies.

Mentors in this aspirational reality disrupt the conventional, linear wisdom that views teacher education and early career mentoring as two distinct developmental entities by seeing them as interwoven parts of the same process. The early career teacher is still being educated, but they also bring their own skills and confidences to the classroom. In this view, mentorship takes on dialogic forms in which the mentor also expects to learn from the practice and reflections of the mentee, as well as from the process of mentoring itself. It also means that mentors' expectations are not unduly limited by preconceptions of novicehood, but rather they are open to discovering that new professionals may have instincts and intuitions which defy their relative limited experience. Conversely, this perturb-ing of traditional teacher-education into teaching-profession lineation also challenges the idea that those novices have arrived professionally by acknowledging that the early years of teaching are merely a stage in a career-long learning journey. Dichotomies like trained/untrained or qualified/unqualified become less important than questions such as how do new teachers respond when faced with certain dilemmas? How useful are their responses? And what assumptions or values underpin them?

As well as supporting the development of conscious competence and deliberate, adaptive practice, mentors operating within a professional judgement framework also appreciate the value and necessity of pedagogical habit forming. The busy and complex nature of classrooms and classroom teaching and learning does not afford teachers the luxury of being individually attentive to every unique event, and therefore they must form and draw on established habits to operate efficiently. Judgement 1 plays a key role in this by encouraging an evaluative focus on the usefulness (or otherwise) of previous judgements so that the most productive can be stored for future reference.

Cautions: can you have too much of a good thing?

I have emphasised several times through the book that a focus on judgement need not come at the expense of consideration for competency indicators, professional standards or just good lesson planning. They are not mutually exclusive. I would go as far as to posit that competencies are made more meaningful when expressed using the language of judgement (see Chapter 5). However, the balance in this relationship is important. Too much of anything can be a bad thing and in this final section of the book I want to temper any over-exuberance for professional judgement with a handful of cautionary notes.

A call for more judgement is not a call to throw out structures

Throughout the book I have made the case for the value of equipping trainee and novice teachers with the tools and approval to rehearse their professional judgements. However, this should not be limitless or come at the expense of close attention to learning ways of planning engaging, well-resourced, thought-out, well-paced and carefully assessed lessons. In making the case for teachers learning to improvise in the classroom, I am not making the case for winging it. As has been pointed out repeatedly, classrooms are complex, as are the learning and teaching within them, and without mechanisms for reducing that complexity into manageable forms learning may become less, rather than more, likely. A well-structured lesson plan showing the planned destinations for learning and highlighting events, processes and resources which will support the journey is an essential component of classroom learning. Gert Biesta's (2009) 'enabling constraints', mentioned in Chapter 3, play an important role in this by imposing complexity-reducing structure onto teaching and learning, making the unmanageable and potentially chaotic feasible and productive. In fact, in Biesta's vision of enabling constraints, the constraints do not simply suppress complexity but actually unlock potential. In a similar way, professional judgement (category 1 or 2) is at its most potent and useful when exercised within a clear framework.

In Chapter 2, I referred to the jazz musician who repeatedly deviates from and returns to the main motif during a performance. Musical improvisation is extremely challenging, and somewhat meaningless, without structural anchors like a baseline or a chord progression. Similarly, teaching can quickly unravel and become inconsistent and illogical when not underpinned reliably by features of effective planning (activation of prior knowledge, building on conceptual understanding, demonstration and modelling, pace and timings, questioning and assessment). The same can be said of rubrics which structure professional standards and competencies. I have had the privilege of mentoring numerous highly intuitive trainee teachers who operate fluently and instinctively in the classroom, but whose lessons unravelled due to a lack of preparedness and planning. The structures of ITE curricula and early career frameworks, if skilfully applied, can play an important role in turning such trainees into expert classroom practitioners. However, I have also argued in Chapter 2 that pressures of school placement expectations and assessment structures can have a stifling effect on trainees' ability to rehearse and develop their judgement. Whether structured for lesson planning or descriptions of ideal practice, the language of decisional judgement can hold emerging professionals to account, provide a basis for reflection and empower with a sense of autonomy and professional trust. The question is not 'are structures necessary to the development of teacher expertise?' (clearly, they are), but rather 'how can structures be articulated to enable expertise to flourish?' Trainees and novices with the instincts and confidence to improvise, think on their feet or make mistakes must also be shaped professionally by structural anchors in policy and curricula.

A licence to judge should unfold gradually

Following on from the assertion that structures are a necessary prerequisite to the development of professional judgement, teacher educators and school mentors should also recognise that a novice's licence to judge should escalate incrementally. Judging the readiness of novices to adopt the skills and responsibilities associated with professional judgement is itself not an exact science and requires careful consideration, and perhaps some trial and error. Allowing novices too much licence before they have developed the confidence and competence to adapt to the dynamism of teaching poses risks not only to pupil learning, but also to novices themselves. Confidence to follow one's instinct, believe in one's emerging expertise and learn from mistakes can be undermined by failure to manage too many variables. Increased opportunities for rehearsing judgement should therefore be afforded sensitively and gradually. The models for judgements 1 and 2 presented in this book can support this because they encourage a focus on reflection as a mediator of professional judgement. In addition to a novice's performance in the classroom, their level of reflectiveness and their ability to adapt in light of reflection will give fairly reliable indicators of their readiness to judge. In judging a trainee or novice teacher's readiness to rehearse their judgement, mentors might reflect on whether they demonstrate the following traits.

- » Honest and realistic in reflections on their teaching.
- » Noticing the consequences of their teaching actions.
- » Open about mistakes and failures.
- » Flexibility in thinking about ways of responding to challenges or failures.
- » Knowledge of their limitations and willingness to seek support.
- » Keenness to follow their instincts.
- » Thorough lesson planning.
- » A tendency to deviate from their plans at times.

Where these traits are not evident, mentors may use them as a starting point for reflection and discussion about ways of stimulating professional judgement.

Final thoughts

I began the introduction to the book with a prediction that despite rapid recent advancements in artificial intelligence technologies and the emergence of impressive decision-making machine learning capabilities in the early part of the twenty-first century, teaching will never become automated. The core elements which tessellate to create teaching and learning contexts (pupils, teachers, classrooms, curriculum and culture) interact in ways which are simply too complex and dynamic to be managed algorithmically. A central argument running through the book has been that while structures can have a very useful routinising effect on the dynamic nature of classroom teaching and learning, no amount of structure can eliminate the dynamic qualities of learning collectives. As noted in Chapter 3, even the most tightly organised classrooms are characterised by a mix of what Radford (2008) calls ‘*clockishness*’ and ‘*cloudishness*’. Their complexity cannot be reduced to zero, meaning that some degree of adaptive expertise will always be a requirement in teaching. This means that classroom-based (and even online and virtual) learning will always need teachers to be decision-making agents.

However, as I have argued throughout the book, whether improvised or well-reasoned professional judgement cannot be taken for granted from trainee and novice teachers; it must be nurtured. Teachers at all career stages must be both permitted and sufficiently accomplished to take up that mantle of agency and to act upon it. Eaude (2012) argues that the professional status necessary to enable this permission and expertise is unlikely to come from policymakers. While I agree with him that changes must come from within the profession and share his frustration at the stubbornly slow movement of policy in this direction, I believe that a mixture of bottom-up and top-down change represents the best hope for the enshrining of professional judgement in teaching. In my view, articulations in policy are necessary if teaching and teacher development are to undergo the desirable shift to become more judgement-orientated. How likely this is in the near to medium term is anyone's guess. In the meantime, however, I support Eaude's call for teachers, and their teachers and mentors, to loudly and frequently articulate the complexities of teachers' work and the centrality of professional judgement.

REFERENCES

Acquah, E, Palonen, T, Laine, K and Lehtinen, E (2014) Social Status and Social Behaviour among First Graders. *Scandinavian Journal of Educational Research*, 58(1): 73–92.

Adams, R (2019) Academies and Free Schools Underperform in SATs, Figures Show. *The Guardian*. 13 December. [online] Available at: www.theguardian.com/education/2019/dec/13/academies-and-free-schools-underperform-in-sats-figures-show (accessed 29 July 2023).

Alberta Education (2023) Teaching Quality Standard. Alberta Government. [online] Available at: https://open.alberta.ca/publications/teaching-quality-standard (accessed 14 September 2023).

Arnold, R and Wade, J (2015) A Definition of Systems Thinking: A Systems Approach. *Procedia Computer Science*, 44: 669–78.

Australian Institute for Teaching and School Leadership Limited (AITSL) (2018) *Australian Professional Standards for Teachers (PST)*. Melbourne: AITSL.

BBC (2019) *Primary League Tables: How Did Your School Do?* [online] Available at: www.bbc.co.uk/news/education-50749093 (accessed 29 July 2023).

Beck, C and Kosnik, C (2002) Components of a Good Practicum Placement: Student Teacher Perceptions. *Teacher Education Quarterly*, 29(2): 81–98.

Berliner, D (2004) Describing the Behavior and Documenting the Accomplishments of Expert Teachers. *Bulletin of Science, Technology & Society*, 24(3): 200–12.

Biesta, G (2009) Theorising Learning through Complexity: An Educational Critique. A Response to Ton Jorg's Pragmatic View. *Complicity: An International Journal of Complexity and Education*, 6(1): 28–33.

Blatchford, P, Pellegrini, A and Baines, E (2015) Peer Relations and School Learning. In Blatchford, P, Pellegrini, A and Baines, E (eds) *The Child at School: Interactions with Peers and Teachers* (pp 148–72). London: Routledge.

Brest, P and Hamilton-Krieger, L (2010) *Problem Solving, Decision Making and Professional Judgement: A Guide for Lawyers and Policy Makers*. Oxford: Oxford University Press.

Burn, K, Hagger, H and Mutton, T (2015) *Beginning Teachers' Learning: Making Experience Count*. St Albans: Critical Publishing.

Burn, K, Mutton, T and Thompson, I (eds) (2023) *Practical Theorising in Teacher Education*. London: Routledge.

Burns, A and Knox, J (2011) Classrooms as Complex Adaptive Systems: A Relational Model. *The Electronic Journal for English as a Second Language*, 15(1): 1–25.

Campbell, S and Dunleavy, T (2016) Connecting University Course Work and Practitioner Knowledge through Mediated Field Experiences. *Teacher Education Quarterly*, 43(3): 49–70.

Canovi, A, Kumpulainen, A and Molinari, L (2019) The Dynamics of Class Mood and Student Agency in Classroom Interactions. *Journal of Classroom Interaction*, 54(1): 4–25.

Ciotti, P (1983) Freaked Out by Technology: A Student of the '60s Takes a New Look at What Moved the New Left. *Reason: Free Minds and Free Markets* (August edition 1983, pp 34–7).

Clark, C and Yinger, R (1987) Teacher Planning. In Calderhead, J (ed) *Exploring Teacher Thinking* (pp 84–103). London: Cassell Education Limited.

Claxton, G (2000) The Anatomy of Intuition. In Ackinson, T and Claxton, G (eds) *Intuitive Practice: On the Value of Not Always Knowing What One is Doing* (pp 32–52). Buckingham: Open University Press.

Coles, C (2002) Developing Professional Judgement. *Journal of Continuing Education in the Health Professions*, 22(1): 3–10.

Dalke, A, Cassidy, K, Grobstein, P and Blank, D (2007) Emergent Pedagogy: Learning to Enjoy the Uncontrollable and Make it Productive. *Journal of Educational Change*, 8 (2): 111–30.

Davis, B (2004) *Inventions in Teaching: A Genealogy.* Mahwah, NJ: Lawrence Erlbaum Associates.

Davis, B and Sumara, D (2006) *Complexity and Education: Enquiries into Learning, Teaching and Research.* Abingdon: Routledge.

Department for Education (DfE) (2011) *The Teachers' Standards.* DfE. [online] Available at: www.gov.uk/government/publications/teachers-standards (accessed 29 July 2023).

Department for Education (DfE) (2019a) Early Career Framework. [online] Available at: https://assets.publishing.service.gov.uk/government/uploads/system/uploads/attachment_data/file/978358/Early-Career_Framework_April_2021.pdf (accessed 29 July 2023).

Department for Education (DfE) (2019b) ITT Core Content Framework. [online] Available at: https://assets.publishing.service.gov.uk/government/uploads/system/uploads/attachment_data/file/974307/ITT_core_content_framework_.pdf (accessed 29 July 2023).

Department for Education (DfE) (2021a) *Statutory Framework for the Early Years Foundation Stage.* [online] Available at: https://assets.publishing.service.gov.uk/government/uploads/system/uploads/attachment_data/file/974907/EYFS_framework_-_March_2021.pdf (accessed 29 July 2023).

Department for Education (DfE) (2021b) *The Teachers' Standards.* [online] Available at: https://assets.publishing.service.gov.uk/government/uploads/system/uploads/attachment_data/file/1040274/Teachers__Standards_Dec_2021.pdf (accessed 29 July 2023).

Derrida, J (1998) *Limited Inc.* Evanston, IL: Northwestern University Press.

Dewey, J (1960) *The Quest for Certainty.* Minneapolis, MN: Capricorn Editions.

Dezutter, S (2011) Professional Improvisation and Teacher Education: Opening the Conversation. In Sawyer, R K (ed) *Structure and Improvisation in Creative Teaching* (pp 27–50). Cambridge: Cambridge University Press.

Doll, W (1989) Complexity in the Classroom. *Educational Leadership*, 46(September): 65–70.

Doll, W (1993) *A Post-Modern Perspective on Curriculum.* New York: Teachers College Press.

Dunlosky, J and Metcalfe, J (2009) *Metacognition.* London: Sage.

Dunn, T and Shriner, C (1999) Deliberate Practice in Teaching: What Teachers Do for Self-Improvement. *Teaching and Teacher Education*, 15(6): 631–51.

Dyson, A (1987) The Value of 'Time Off Task': Young Children's Spontaneous Talk and Deliberate Text. *Harvard Educational Review*, 57(4): 396–421.

Eaude, T (2012) *How Do Expert Primary Class Teachers Really Work? A Critical Guide for Teachers, Headteachers and Teacher Educators.* Exeter: Critical Publishing.

Education Council New Zealand (2017) *Our Code our Standards: Code of Professional Responsibility and Standards for the Teaching Profession.* Wellington: Education Council.

Eraut, M (2000) The Intuitive Practitioner: A Critical Overview. In Ackinson, T and Claxton, G (eds) *Intuitive Practice: On the Value of Not Always Knowing What One is Doing* (pp 255–68). Buckingham: Open University Press.

Erickson, F (1996) Going for the Zone: The Social and Cognitive Ecology of Teacher-Student Interaction in Classroom Conversations. In Hicks, D (ed) *Discourse, Learning and Schooling* (pp 29–62). Cambridge: Cambridge University Press.

Ericsson, K and Moxley, J (2012) The Expert Performance Approach and Deliberate Practice: Some Potential Implications for Studying Creative Performance in Organizations. In Mumford M (ed) *Handbook of Organizational Creativity* (pp 141–67). Cambridge, MA: Academic Press.

Fraher, R (1984) Learning a New Art: Suggestions for Beginning Teachers. In Gullete, M M (ed) *The Art and Craft of Teaching* (pp 116–27). Cambridge, MA: Harvard University Press.

Furlong, J (2000) Intuition and the Crisis in Teacher Professionalism. In Ackinson, T and Claxton, G (eds) *Intuitive Practice: On the Value of Not Always Knowing What One is Doing* (pp 15–31). Buckingham: Open University Press.

Furlong, J (2015) *Teaching Tomorrow's Teachers: Options for the Future of Initial Teacher Education in Wales.* A Report to Huw Lewis, AM, Minister for Education and Skills. March 2015. Oxford: Oxford University Press.

Grimmett, P and MacKinnon, A (1992) Craft Knowledge and the Education of Teachers. In Grant, G (ed) *Review of Research in Education* (vol 18, pp 385–456). Washington DC: American Educational Research Association.

Haggis, T (2008) Knowledge Must be Contextual. In Mason, M (ed) *Complexity and the Philosophy of Education* (pp 150–68). Chichester: Wiley-Blackwell.

Hammond Stoughton, E (2007) 'How Will I Get Them to Behave?' Pre Service Teachers Reflect on Classroom Management. *Teaching and Teacher Education*, 23(7): 1024–37.

Hara, M and Sherbine, K (2018) Be[com]ing a Teacher in Neoliberal Times: The Possibilities of Visioning for Resistance in Teacher Education. *Policy Futures in Education*, 16(6): 669–90.

Hardman, M (2010) Is Complexity Theory Useful in Describing Classroom Learning? In *Proceedings of the European Conference on Educational Research (ECER)* (pp 23–7). August 2010. Helsinki, Finland.

Hargreaves, A and Fullan, M (2012) *Professional Capital: Transforming Teaching in Every School.* London: Routledge.

Harrison, J, Lawson, T and Wortley, A (2005) Facilitating the Professional Learning of New Teachers through Critical Reflection on Practice during Mentoring Meetings. *European Journal of Teacher Education*, 28(3): 267–92.

Heilbronn, R (2008) *Teacher Development and the Development of Practical Judgement.* London: Continuum.

Helleve, I, Eide, L and Ulvik, M (2021) Case-based Teacher Education Preparing for Diagnostic Judgement. *European Journal of Teacher Education*, 46(1): 50–66. https://doi.org/10.1080/02619768.2021.1900112

Hendrickx, M, Mainhard, T, Oudman, S, Boor-Klip, H and Breklemans, M (2017) Teacher Behavior and Peer Liking and Disliking: The Teacher as a Social Referent for Peer Status. *Journal of Educational Psychology*, 109(4): 546–58.

Holdhus, K, Høisæter, S, Mæland, K, Vangsnes, V, Steinar Engelsen, K, Espeland, M and Espeland, Å (2016) Improvisation in Teaching and Education—Roots and Applications. *Cogent Education*, 3(1): 1–17.

Hoyle, E and John, P (1995) *Professional Knowledge and Professional Practice.* London: Cassell.

Ipsos MORI (2015) *Veracity Index.* London: Ipsos MORI Social Research Institute.

Johnson, L (2016) *A Complexity Context to North Carolina Charter School Classroom Interactions and Climate: Achievement Gap Impacts.* Doctor of Education (EdD) dissertation (unpublished). Faculty of the Graduate School of Education and Human Development of the George Washington University.

Jordan, M, Kleinsasser, R and Roe, M (2014) Cautionary Tales: Teaching, Accountability, and Assessment. *The Education Forum*, 78(3): 323–37.

Karlsson Lohmander, M (2015) Bridging 'the Gap' – Linking Workplace-based and University-based Learning in Preschool Teacher Education in Sweden. *Early Years*, 35(2): 168–83.

Kember, D and Leung, D Y (2005) The Influence of the Teaching and Learning Environment on the Development of Generic Capabilities Needed for a Knowledge-based Society. *Learning Environments Research*, 8(3): 245–66.

Kirk, A (2020) Primary School League Table: Search and Compare the Best Primary Schools in Your Area. *The Telegraph*. 16 April. [online] Available at: www.telegraph.co.uk/education-and-careers/0/primary-school-league-table-search-compare-best-primary-schools1/ (accessed 29 July 2023).

Knight, B (2017) The Evolving Codification of Teachers' Work: Policy, Politics and the Consequences of Pursuing Quality Control in Initial Teacher Education. *Teacher Education Advancement Network (TEAN)*, 9(1): 4–13.

Knight, B (2022a) Classroom as Complex Adaptive System (CAS): Credible Framing, Useful Metaphor or Mis-designation? *International Journal of Complexity in Education*, 3(1): 33–60.

Knight, B (2022b) Complex Adaptive System Behaviours in Small Group Interaction: A Year 4 Classroom Case Study of Learning as 'Emergence'. Thesis. University of the West of England. [online] Available at: https://uwe-repository.worktribe.com/output/9030663 (accessed 29 July 2023).

Langer-Osuna, J (2018) Productive Disruptions: Rethinking the Role of Off-Task Interactions in Collaborative Mathematics Learning. *Education Sciences*, 8(2): 1–11. https://doi.org/10.3390/educsci8020087

Lizzio, A and Wilson, K (2004) Action Learning in Higher Education: An Investigation of Its Potential to Develop Professional Capability. *Studies in Higher Education*, 29(4): 469–88.

Lizzio, A and Wilson, K (2007) Developing Critical Professional Judgement: The Efficacy of a Self-managed Reflective Process. *Studies in Continuing Education*, 29(3): 277–93.

Lobman, C (2011) Improvising within the System: Creating New Teacher Performances in Inner-City Schools. In Sawyer, R K (ed) *Structure and Improvisation in Creative Teaching* (pp 73–93). New York: Cambridge University Press.

Mæland, K and Espeland, M (2017) Teachers' Conceptions of Improvisation in Teaching: Inherent Human Quality or a Professional Teaching Skill? *Education Inquiry*, 8(3): 192–208.

Meijer, P, de Graaf, G and Meirink, J (2011) Key Experiences in Student Teachers' Development. *Teachers and Teaching*, 17(1): 115–29.

Menter, I (2016) Helga Eng lecture, 2015: What is a Teacher in the 21st Century and What Does a 21st Century Teacher Need to Know? *Acta Didactica Norge*, 10(2): 11–25.

National Foundation for Educational Research (NFER) (2020) *Teacher Autonomy: How Does It Relate to Job Satisfaction and Retention?* Slough: NFER.

Ndaruhutse, S, Jones, C and Riggall, A (2019) *Why Systems Thinking is Important for the Education Sector*. Berkshire: Education Development Trust.

Ollerton, M (2014) Differentiation in Mathematics Classrooms. *Association of Teachers of Mathematics (ATM) Journal*, May 2014: 43–46.

Pattinson, R (2020) Pain in the Class: Primary School 'Axes Teacher Because Kids' SATs Results Were Too Good'. *The Sun*. 11 February. [online] Available at: www.thesun.co.uk/news/10944050/primary-school-axes-teacher-sats-results-too-good/ (accessed 29 July 2023).

Philip, T (2019) Principled Improvisation to Support Novice Teacher Learning. *Teachers College Record*, 121(6): 1–32.

Pollard, A (2008) *Reflective Teaching: Evidence-informed Professional Practice* (3rd edition). London: Continuum.

Pollard, A (ed) (2010) *Professionalism and Pedagogy: A Contemporary Opportunity: A Commentary by TLRP and GTCE*. London: TLRP.

Postman, N and Weingartner, C (1969) *Teaching as a Subversive Activity*. New York: Delacorte Press.

Preble, D (1973) *Man Creates Art Creates Man*. Berkeley, CA: McCutchan Publishing Corp.

Priestley, M, Biesta, G and Robinson, S (2015) *Teacher Agency: An Ecological Approach*. London: Bloomsbury.

Quirk-Marku, C and Hulme, M (2017) Re-making Teacher Professionalism in England: Localism and Social Responsibility. *RASE: Revista de la Asociación de Sociología de la Educación*, 10(3): 347–62.

Radford, M (2008) Complexity and Truth in Educational Research. In Mason, M (ed) *Complexity and the Philosophy of Education* (pp 137–49). Chichester: Wiley-Blackwell.

Richmond, B (1994) Systems Thinking/System Dynamics: Let's Just Get On with It. *System Dynamics Review*, 10(2–3): 135–57.

Rogers, T (2016) Teaching is Incredibly Difficult to Master. It is a Craft; The Classroom is the Canvas and the Outcome is the Art. *Times Educational Supplement (TES)*. [online] Available at: www.tes.com/magazine/archive/teaching-incredibly-difficult-master-it-craft-classroom-canvas-and-outcome-art (accessed 29 July 2023).

Sawyer, K (2004) Creative Teaching: Collaborative Discussion as Disciplined Improvisation. *Educational Researcher*, 33(2): 12–20.

Schön, D (1983) *The Reflective Practitioner: How Professionals Think in Action*. New York: Basic Books.

Schön, D (1987) *Jossey-Bass Higher Education Series. Educating the Reflective Practitioner: Toward a New Design for Teaching and Learning in the Professions*. San Francisco, CA: Jossey-Bass.

Schön, D (1991) *The Reflective Practitioner: How Professionals Think in Action*. London: Routledge.

Shulman, L (2004) *The Wisdom of Practice: Essays on Teaching, Learning and Learning to Teach*. San Francisco, CA: Jossey-Bass.

Sinnema, C, Aitken, G and Meyer, F (2017) Capturing the Complex, Context-Bound and Active Nature of Teaching through Inquiry-oriented Standards for Teaching. *Journal of Teacher Education*, 68(1): 9–27.

Stephenson, J and Weil, S (1992) *Quality in Learning: A Capability Approach to Higher Education*. London: Kogan Page.

Storey, B and Butler, J (2010) Ecological Thinking and TGfU: Understanding Games as Complex Adaptive Systems. In Butler, J and Griffin, L (eds) *More Teaching Games for Understanding: Moving Globally* (pp 139–54). Champaign, IL: Human Kinetics.

Strom, K and Mitchell Viesca, K (2020) Towards a Complex Framework of Teacher Learning-Practice. *Professional Development in Education*, 47(2–3): 209–24.

Sullivan, J (2009) *Emergent Learning: The Power of Complex Adaptive Systems in the Classroom*. PhD thesis (unpublished). Department of Teacher Education, Special Education, Curriculum and Instruction, Lynch School of Education. Boston College.

Taylor, B and Whittaker, A (2018) Professional Judgement and Decision Making in Social Work. *Journal of Social Work Practice*, 32(2): 105–9. https://doi.org/10.1080/02650533.2018.1462780

Thorndike, E (1910) The Contribution of Psychology to Education. *Journal of Educational Psychology*, 1(1): 5–12.

Tom, A (1980) Teaching as a Moral Craft: A Metaphor for Teaching and Teacher Education. *Curriculum Inquiry*, 10(3): 317–23.

Tomlinson, S (1997) Edward Lee Thorndike and John Dewey on the Science of Education. *Oxford Review of Education*, 23(3): 365–83.

Tripp, D (1993) *Critical Incidents in Teaching: Developing Professional Judgement.* London: Routledge/Falmer.

Ulvik, M and Smith, K (2011) What Characterises a Good Practicum in Teacher Education? *Education Enquiry,* 2(3): 517–36.

Wallace, M, Rust, J and Jolly, E (2021) 'It's All There.' Entanglements of Teacher Preparation and Induction. *Professional Development in Education,* 47(2–3): 406–20.

Winch, C, Oancea, A and Orchard, J (2015) The Contribution of Educational Research to Teachers' Professional Learning – Philosophical Understandings. *Oxford Review of Education,* 41(2): 202–16.

Witt, M, Lewis, F and Knight, B (2022) 'I Wasn't Worried Because I Wasn't Being Judged': The Development of Pre-service Teacher Professional Capital, Pedagogical Instinct and Discretionary Judgement during an Overseas Teaching Placement. *Teaching and Teacher Education,* 112(2): 1–11.

Wong, M and Wong, J (2014) The Classroom as a System. *Educational Technology,* 54(5): 53–55.

Yin, J (2019) Connecting Theory and Practice in Teacher Education: English-as-a-Foreign-Language Pre-service Teachers' Perceptions of Practicum Experience. *Innovation and Education,* 1(4): 1–8.

INDEX

Note: Page numbers in **bold** and *italics* denote tables and figures, respectively.